Back Where We Belong

by
James Knowles

AuthorHouse™ UK Ltd.
500 Avebury Boulevard
Central Milton Keynes, MK9 2BE
www.authorhouse.co.uk
Phone: 08001974150

© 2008 James Knowles. All rights reserved.

No part of this book may be reproduced, stored in a retrieval system, or transmitted by any means without the written permission of the author.

First published by AuthorHouse 8/1/2008

ISBN: 978-1-4389-0528-0 (sc)

Printed in the United States of America
Bloomington, Indiana

This book is printed on acid-free paper.

Now, this was one of those conversations that gets people thinking. Rob turned to me on the coach in London and said, "Why don't you write a book?". Immediately I thought "why not". I'd already written a log of all the games- why not let others know of my tales?

It was 11.57 and we were slowly making our way back from a defeat at Charlton. Glum faces. We couldn't afford to lose three points tonight. Bloody linesman. Cost us a vital draw. It's always the same story. Us fans can always find someone else to blame.

I've been supporting Stoke since my first match in 1993. I was lucky enough to go to my first few games in that season, when we won the Division Two Championship. The likes of Bruce Grobbelaar graced their presence in a Stoke shirt that year. Surely every season was like this? Top names, winning games comfortably, silverware. How wrong could I be?

I go to matches with various people in my life. Firstly, there is my Dad, Thomas. It was his fault that I have caught the bug that is Stoke City Football Club. Dad was born in Trent Vale, just a small walk from the old Victoria Ground. With nobody else to support, Stoke was the obvious choice.

I will be eternally grateful for this. A father passing something special down to his son like the love of a football club is something money cannot buy. It will never leave me.

There is also his sister, my Aunty, Isabelle. She combines betting on horses with coming to the Britannia Stadium on a cold winter's day. She has been a season ticket holder with us for the past five years and is always good company. Sitting down and soaking in the play before giving us all a comprehensive report at the end of the 90 minutes.

Finally, there is Rob. I met Rob on a coach at a famous visit to Elland Road last season. We won 4-0. If anything is going to strike up a friendship it is going to be a handsome victory against recent European Cup semi-finalists. I now keep in contact with Rob on a daily basis, meeting up with him at all away matches.

Last year I took the liberty to travel to Australia to watch the fateful cricket team get stuffed in the Ashes. It was an experience I will never forget, but you cannot beat that feeling on a Saturday. That buzz. YOUR team is playing. Nothing else matters. All you care about is those 22 men running around kicking a leather round ball. Sounds dead simple really.

In my time as a Stokie, I have done my fair share of travelling. My first two years saw me housed in Lancashire before flying down the M6, past Stoke and to Gloucestershire for twelve years of my life.

A few years back we decided four hours driving for home matches was becoming a little too much so we moved to Eccleshall, a mere 20 minutes away from the sacred home of Stoke City. It was strange leaving the house for the first time at quarter to 2 on a Saturday. In the past I'd already been in the car for a couple of hours by that time!

The close proximity was fantastic. I could go to "Meet the Manager" evenings, watch the reserve team play and also pick up the local newspaper to read about all things Stoke City.

At the end of the 2006-2007 season, on one of my frequent pilgrimages back to my old stomping ground in Gloucestershire, I met a wonderful young lady, Alexis. The only problem is she lives in Stratford-upon-Avon. I'm back to square one! Long journeys to the Brit for a home match again. It's like being in a time-warp!

Not to worry. There's more to life than football. So I'm told.

2006/2007 Season overview

This is a copy of an email I sent to Rob following a 1-1 draw against QPR on the final day of the season which meant we missed out on the play-offs.

Rob,

I was going to email you on Sunday night, and again yesterday. Then I realised I was too depressed to type. It was a shame for such a great season just to end like that. Although we were far from our best on Sunday, we did have enough chances to win 5-1. You look back at Fuller off the line, Martin hitting the post and bottling the one-on-one, Matteo (from one yard) and a couple of half chances for Russell and Pericard. Add to that the Higgy disallowed goal (probably off side, but could have gone our way). Put those together and you have a few goals. Also, the QPR goal was terrible to concede- a real mistake, but hey ho...next season. Like you, I can't quite believe the season is over, it is strange. I was so confident we would have another three games it is like someone from the FA has decided to end the season early!!

As for the season. It has been a fantastic season. We have come a long way in 12 months. Think how meaningless the last 10 or so games last season were, yet our last 10 games have been cup finals this season. We have the right chairman and right manager in place, who seem to be a dream team and are here for the long haul. I also believe our Chief Exec (Tony Scholes) is a good bloke, despite what people say. He seems willing to listen to the fans and this can only be a good thing. I will quickly run down the playing staff:

Simmo- Overall a decent campaign, but some costly errors (Southampton, Preston, QPR, Wolves). At this level a great keeper though and we must keep hold of him.

Zakuani- Played more than I thought he would. A good defensive player, but we have seen his last game I fear.

Higginbotham-Class.

Fortune-Better than Duberry, but now Charlton are down I don't think we will keep him. He will start next season as Charlton's first choice centre back.

Griffin-Not as good as people make out. First loan spell turned out very well. Perhaps injury has meant we haven't seen the best of him second time round. Looks like he is coming permanently which I can live with.

Dickinson-A good cover for Griff, and could push him next season. A few errors of judgement (too much enthusiasm), namely at Sunderland.

Hill- An OK half season, probably on his way though, which will be a shame.

Eustace- Come into his old form recently but I do fear that he won't get a new contract. His wave at the end of the QPR match could be the last time we see him.

Bangoura- Simply awful, keep him in Belgium!!!

Sidibe- Love him to bits. I would go as far as saying he is my favourite player at Stoke. His goal at QPR summed him up. Great season, a few more goals than we expected and a new contract...perfect!

Fuller- The one player who makes you get on the edge of your seat. Frightning on form, frustrating when not. If he sorts his temper out then he could be the man to take us up next year.

Sweeney- Drink driving sums him up. Although, like you say, first couple of months of the season he was one of our better players.

Pericard- Hopeless. Apparently not fit, so maybe a bit better to come next year?!!

Hendrie- His form has tailed off but no doubt he was a class signing. Don't think he will come back though.

Diao- I am optimistic he will re-sign which would be a great coup. He has been fantastic, although sometimes slows down the play too much.

Matteo- Solid signing. Not an exciting player so gets some stick (especially on Sunday when he was very poor). However, look at who he replaced...Brammer!

Martin- His two best appearances have been when Hendrie has gone off injured (Plymouth & QPR). Decent promise but hasn't quite lived up to it yet. It would be nice to get him for another season, but his lack of appearances might play against us in our quest to get him for next year.

Lawrence- Hot and cold like you say. However, who is Luke Chadwick? When was the last time you heard his name?!! It shows how well Liam has done- especially the last 4 games or so. Important he comes back injury free next year.

Delap- Good performance at Leeds then THAT break. Not sure how good he will be after the injury, but another body to add to the squad.

Paterson- An eager player, but you have to feel sorry for him after the Cardiff miss. Scored a decent goal at Sheff Wed, more to come next year?

Rooney- Not many chances this season, and no play offs for him at Yeovil. A bit of a wasted season to be honest, but hopefully more time on the pitch next year.

That's my evaluation of the season. Next year could be historic. There is plenty of optimism around the fans but like Lou Macari says, it will be far from easy.

Speak to you soon

James

Pre-season (part one)

Stoke's traditional curtain raiser comes against local side Newcastle Town. We have a good working relationship with them, with our reserve side using the Lyme Valley Stadium for half of their fixtures throughout the season.

The visit of Stoke, sees the lowly side pick up some much needed cash for the season ahead. Despite driving rain, 1,966 turned up to see Stoke for the first time in a few months. It is the first opportunity to see any new signings, and is always good value to see some trialists in a Stoke shirt. This year's trialist was a former Bolton defender going by the exotic name of Ndiwa Lord-Kangana who performed fairly well. Our only new signing was former loanee Jon Parkin, which had been on the cards throughout the summer.

Another wonderful thing about the Newcastle Town match is that we field two different line-ups in both halves of the match. The first half team won 2-1 with a brace from Ricardo Fuller, while the second half side faired better, polishing off the scoreline to finish 5-1 (Vincent Pericard, Liam Lawrence and Robert Garrett with the further goals).

So, football is back. It feels like it has never left us. Onto the second match of pre-season.

The next fixture was in a few days time about an hour away at Macclesfield Town. The rain hadn't stopped all week, and there was a strong doubt as to whether the match would actually take place. Despite numerous pitch inspections, the pitch was deemed safe enough, and we took our position as visiting supporters on a standing terrace behind the goal with no roof. I got absolutely soaked! I made the journey on my own, but we all know each other as Stokies, so found some people to huddle with and keep warm!

We fell behind early on through a well worked goal from the home side. This allowed the boo-boys who had made the trip from Stoke to voice their anger at the lack of transfer activity. I must admit, I was becoming fairly frustrated at the shortage of new faces, but falling behind in a friendly at Macclesfield is hardly going to shape your entire season!!

Ironically, it was our only new signing to date, Jon Parkin who got us level. A powerful header saw him score against the side who used to adore him a few years ago. The one sour note was seeing Rory Delap, who was making his first steps back from a broken leg, limp off. Hopefully it won't be bad enough to prevent him from travelling to Austria.

27 July 2007. Real Madrid (neutral).

An incredible journey. Two weeks ago, our director of football John Rudge announced we are going to play Real Madrid in a friendly. I wasn't going to pass up this opportunity. I managed to drag fellow Stokie Mark, from the warehouse at work to join me on the voyage to Austria.

This wasn't an ordinary friendly. No. At 1.15AM we left my house without any sleep. It was a case of quickly organising time off work and jetting down to Stansted airport for one of the most prestigious friendlies in the club's history.

With matchsticks keeping our eyes open, we arrived at Stansted just as the sun was rising and flew across to Salzburg. Once there, it was time to get the old German dictionary out. Now despite my best efforts, I have completely failed to grasp the German language, which made life extremely difficult when trying to explain we were trying to get over to a small village called Irdning.

We caught what we thought was a direct train through to the village but were shocked when we were ushered off the vehicle and onto a bus. Having sat on the bus for about an hour and a half, and seen the umpteenth mountain roll by, we reached our destination (via a €10 taxi journey).

We had heard reports that the match was close to a sell out, so we were dumped at the ground and bought our tickets. Excellent, tickets bought (for a bargain price of €12), just seven hours until kick-off!

We had been fortunate enough to have organised accommodation in Irdning (after a week of conversation with the local tourist board). Unfortunately the house we were staying in were completely fluent in just one language, German. Mark and I didn't have a clue what was going on and having smiled our way through a half hour 'chat', we determined where our beds were and then headed off to the bars before reaching the ground.

Wearing our red and white stripes, the locals were extremely confused. Surely it would only be Spaniards at this game? Nobody supports Stoke enough to make the trek do they? OK, I'm a bit of a loser. I would follow Stoke wherever they may be. In fact, I had made this same journey three years ago to watch us lose to Roma. Once it's in your blood, it's there to stay.

Having filled our bellies with the fantastic cuisine on offer- chicken schnitzel washed down with good German ale, we arrived at the ground. We welcomed the Stoke team off the coach, applauding them and treating them as heroes. The sad thing was it was just me and Mark who were doing this. When Real Madrid arrived it was a whole different story. Hundreds of supporters clambered to get a better view of their idols as they were escorted into the ground by police and stewards. To see the likes of Raúl, van Nistelrooy and Cannavaro up close was something I never dreamt of doing.

After all the excitement of that, it was time to get into the ground. Stoke had been allocated a small section, right in the corner of the ground. Uncovered benches, with gravel at our feet. Now, this is unusual!! Last time I was here (with my Dad) it was a free-for-all, with no segregation. It led to some fighting between Stoke and Roma fans which was all a bit embarrassing to be honest. The Austrians had got it right on this occasion. About 100 fans were in the Stoke section (although some I spoke to were English people living in the area). One of the best things was the luxury of sitting in your seat and having a beer, something which has been abolished in recent years in England.

The match was almost a side issue to the day's activities. We gave a good account of ourselves against the side with the most illustrious European history of all time. We lost 2-0 but gave the Spaniards a few scares along the way (and their second goal came from an extremely dodgy penalty).

There was enough time after the match to try out the local 'night-club'. To be perfectly honest, to call this place a night-club was an insult. It was a complete dive, with about three people braving the dance floor. Mark and I quickly exited the place before we saw more of it!!

After a good night's sleep, we headed back to England via Salzburg and arrived back home at 1.00AM on Sunday morning. Exactly two days after we had set off.

Perhaps you are now beginning to realise what a ridiculously passionate fan I am of Stoke City.

"Pitch Invasion!"

"Me and Mark at one of the most picturesque football grounds in the World"

Pre-season (part two)

Having returned from Austria, we had two more friendlies to play. The first came at home at the Britannia Stadium against Aston Villa. Last season, Villa's manager, Martin O'Neill, had been kind enough to lend us Lee Hendrie and Patrik Berger to aid us in our ultimately unsuccessful task of getting promotion.

With the sun shining, and the players wearing a specially designed white kit, we hoped to slay our Premier League opponents. We had invited our next-door neighbour to this match, and as a Villa fan, he came home the happier of us all.

Typically, it was Berger who opened the scoring by firing past Simonsen in goal, and then the speedy Gabriel Agbonlahor outstripped the defence to make it two. Not an embarrassing defeat, but the 7,000 fans who turned up would have expected a little bit more fight from the boys.

Our final pre-season match came on Merseyside at Tranmere Rovers' Prenton Park. In the morning leading up to the match we made two new signings. Richard Cresswell turned his back on Hull, and decided to leave Leeds for us, while we signed Stephen Wright on loan from Sunderland. The Wright signing came with mixed views. It was clear that he was a replacement for the seemingly out-going fans favourite Carl Hoefkens, who had fallen out with the manager. The Hoefkens situation intensified when he was named on the official team-sheet, yet watched the game from the stands. A bizarre thing indeed!

Awful defending handed Tranmere the lead, before a spanking free-kick from their most influential player Steven Davies gave Simonsen no chance.

It was a poor performance, and one which led the bloke infront of me to stand up, and proclaim 'I'd rather be in the pub than watch this rubbish'. He wasn't seen again!

Another fan decided to start interesting chants about how terrible we were. This isn't the best preparation a week before the league season kicks off! A 30 yard free kick from captain Danny Higginbotham wasn't enough to lift the spirits and we left the ground on the end of a 2-1 reverse.

It could be a long season if these performances are anything to go by!

11 August 2007. Cardiff City (away)

The first day of the new football season. A trip to the Welsh capital with the sun beaming down. A beautiful day to watch football. Dad picked me up from Stratford and we drove cross-country to Cardiff. On arrival in Wales we parked the car in the city centre and I wandered off to the ground. I left dad to his own devices, but after my lack of football over the past couple of months I wanted to get there early. I wanted to savour everything that I had missed about a competitive football match.

We even beat the team coach to the ground and after applauding the lads off the bus, I bumped into Cardiff's new signing Robbie Fowler. The Welshmen were extremely optimistic and were ready to start the season off in style against the enemy…Stoke.

Now, despite being miles away geographically, Cardiff and Stoke haven't seen eye to eye in recent years. It all stemmed when their chairman Sam Hammam thought it would be a clever idea to buy Stoke's best players at the time- Graham Kavanagh and Peter Thorne.

It didn't go down well with Stoke fans who decided to start a rivalry with their Welsh counterparts, who were only to happy to return the compliment. Just to make things worse for Cardiff, the year they bought these two stars, we beat them in a Roy of the Rovers play off semi final and duly gained promotion at their expense.

Anyway, the bad blood means that these fixtures are especially spicy- both on the pitch and in the stands. Huge segregation and netting is in place and half of the city's police force seems to be employed at Ninnian Park for a few hours.

Last year, Stoke were cruelly denied a crucial victory after young striker Martin Paterson missed an open goal and Chopra scored for them in the final minutes.

This was Cardiff's first game without Chopra and news filtered through the ground that he had scored a last minute winner for his new side Sunderland in the morning kick off. A bitter pill to swallow for the Welsh supporters. It wasn't that bad, at least they had £5.5 million more in the bank, most of which was spent on Fowler.

Their new hero Fowler was unavailable for this match (something that would be a theme for most of the season) but it was still a formidable task facing the red and white Potters.

In what was seemingly a desperation signing on the eve of the new season, manager Tony Pulis had signed unknown defender Ryan Shawcross from the mighty Manchester United. The young lad was shoved into the heart of the defence alongside last year's player of the season Danny Higginbotham.

What a performance from Ryan. He swung his boot at a corner and the ball nestled into the back of the net. Cue an absolute frenzy amongst the away supporters.

Cardiff is one of only a handful of grounds which allows away fans to stand on terraces. It is a nice draw back to the good old days. Fans jumping around, hugging random people. We are all one- all lost in the moment. Stoke have scored for the first time this season. A release of emotion from all the Stokies present.

It was all going fairly swimmingly for us. Cardiff weren't posing much threat until late in the game, hero Shawcross decided to give away a penalty to hand Cardiff a lifeline.

Alas, our keeper Simonsen made a miraculous double save and the points were safe! The pandemonium in the stands had to be seen to be believed. People falling over in delight, losing breath as they struggle to contain themselves.

The opening day is one of the best days of the year…especially when you are successful. Songs are sung that have been kept in the locker since May and by the end of the match all fans are hoarse having sung at the top of their voices.

After the match, the Welsh police decided to lock us in to avoid any trouble outside, giving time for the Cardiff fans to disperse. We greeted the players as they returned to the pitch for their warm-down with a chorus of our trademark song- Tom Jones' Delilah.

Once allowed out, Dad and I headed off to our car in the centre. Due to the heat, all I was wearing was my crisp, clean and brand new Stoke shirt, so my colours were firmly nailed to the mast. As we turned to our right (in the opposite direction to the official coaches) we were faced with a mob of about 300 Cardiff fans wanting blood.

As it was just me and Dad against this 300 strong crowd, to say we were thankful for the police presence would be a slight understatement.

On closer inspection, the Cardiff fans had got a bit bored of waiting for the Stokies to come out so had decided to have a mini-riot amongst themselves.

With bottles flying in the air, and riot police present, we decided to slip by and walk briskly back to the car until we were abruptly stopped by a drunk man in a Welsh shirt.

We thought the worst until he slurred the words "Let me walk you back to your car. They won't harm you if I'm with you". So not to cause trouble we agreed, and despite the odd traitor remark thrown at the drunk, no grief was caused and we travelled home safely, along with the three points.

14 August 2007. Rochdale (away)

This was the first match that really annoyed Alexis. It fell on Alana's birthday and a huge night had been arranged. Now, Alana (Alexis' sister) happens to be going out with my best mate, Gilley, who is a Sheffield Wednesday fan.

Gilley and I go back a long way, and he is always good for a bit of banter. He has even been good enough to accompany me to Stoke v Sheffield Wednesday ties in the past in the Stoke end….and kept quiet (just)!

It did not go down well that I chose to visit Spotland rather than a night on the tiles in Birmingham.

This was a new ground for me though, I wasn't going to pass up the opportunity of seeing the two teams with the worst cup history in English football battle it out. Going in to the season I had visited 72 of the 92 football league grounds, so the chance to get another one on my list was not going to be passed.

Despite our tremendous victory at Ninnian Park, most Stokies travelled north fully expecting Rochdale to win. Despite them being two divisions below us, we know the script by now. We always lose to lower league opposition in the League Cup!

Spotland is a lovely traditional lower league ground with a bit of standing for the home fans and sporadic seating dotted around the ground, including for the visitors.

Much to the shock of the away fans, that young man Shawcross scored again to give us an early lead. We couldn't believe it!!

Somehow, we were actually in control in the cup. This wasn't part of the script!

Rob, whom my Dad and I had met at the ground, kept expressing his shock. I was literally speechless!! The lead lasted for most of the match, but in the latter stages Rochdale equalised to take the tie into extra time.

This was far from good news for me. I had promised Alexis that I would make the visit to Birmingham after the final whistle to join in with the birthday celebrations. The longer the match went on, the later I would be and the troops would not be happy!

The away fans were getting restless, and there was a bit of verbals going on between midfielder Liam Lawrence and a group of Stokies, which is never nice to see.

Having lost a late goal, we were prepared for what was going to happen. Indeed, Rochdale did score and we were surely out. No! Substitute, and new signing Richard Cresswell went on a bundling run and his shot cannoned in off a defender.

Supporters celebrations were almost one of embarrassment. We had just scraped a penalty shoot-out against a League Two side! Woohoo!

However, the shoot out was still to come and true to form, Stoke lost it. We have only won one shoot out in our history. We managed to knock out non-leaguers Tamworth last year. It truly was a momentous day in the history of our previous manager Johan Boskamp. After debutant keeper Russell Hoult's comic performance, we didn't hold out too much hope that we would do that well. It was sad to see youngster Carl Dickinson miss the crucial kick, but, despite being in tears he still plucked up the courage to applaud the travelling fans, as he always does.

So, out of the cup, and then a long journey late at night to Birmingham. I managed to make it so the first liquid hit my mouth at 1.00 in the morning.

18 August 2007. Charlton Athletic (home).

The first home match of the season. Stokies return to their 'second home' for the first time in a while. It is as though we haven't been away. This game is a bit different from normal. Sky have decided to change the kick-off time to 5.20 on a Saturday evening just to mess everybody's routine up.

It was no great surprise. Charlton are favourites for promotion and Stoke came ever so close to promotion last year. It was one that the neutral would look forward to sitting on the sofa in the evening and relaxing, eating their bangers and mash.

My Mum had decided to come along to the Brit for this one. She is far from a football fan but does her best to get her head around my passion for the game. She puts up with my Dad, merely because he will never change. Stoke is in his blood.

Could Stoke put a spanner in the works and upset the odds against the Londoners? Due to a defensive crisis, we had to call our friends up the road at Wolverhampton and borrow Jody Craddock for a couple of weeks. He came straight into the team and did well on his debut.

Part of our problem in defence was that former loanee Jonathan Fortune turned down a permanent move to the Britannia Stadium and stay at Charlton. Accordingly, it was he who deflected in a free kick to give the visitors the lead.

That undeserved lead only lasted a minute. Our mercurial striker Ricardo Fuller produced a bit of magic. With his back to goal he turned on the edge and fired in a beauty to bring us level. The stadium was alive. The fans had woken up. A goal of real quality had kick started our home campaign and there was more to come.

Four minutes after bringing on the most overweight player seen at the Britannia Stadium, Stoke won the match. Jon Parkin was brought in on loan last season from Hull City, who were struggling at the wrong end of the table. After a horrendous start, he promptly scored three goals in three games before being recalled by his parent club. Pulis decided to shell out £500,000 to obtain his permanent services in the summer. It seemed like money well spent when the man they call the Beast (due to his size) rolled past his defender and calmly stroked the ball home to put the Potters on top of the table.

Six available points in the league, six taken. What a start!

25 August 2007. Southampton (away)

On another very pleasant day, Rob and I travelled down to the South coast on the official coaches. People are every eager when it comes to coach travel. A majority of people turn up about an hour from the expected departure just to guarantee their favourite seat. I'm lazy and leave it to the last minute and let Rob save me a seat so I can sit next to him.

On this occasion there were only a few dotted seats meaning that Rob was forced to sit next to a guy who *had* to sit next to the window because of medical purposes. Have you ever heard such tripe? That's typical of the average Stoke fan- not very accommodating.

Thanks to a very smooth drive, we ended up at the ground way ahead of schedule and duly walked around the perimeter of the ground to gain a real feel of the place.

As we walked off the coach, we gained a young lad who decided it would be a good idea to tag along and almost became our shadow for the remainder of the afternoon. He was a Stokie, so no harm was done.

Having wished former Stokie Wayne Thomas all the best for his prospective Southampton career, we applauded the current Stoke team off the coach.

The match was put into perspective as news filtered through that young QPR striker Ray Jones had been killed in a car crash. Such a waste of a tremendous talent.

Nevertheless, there was a match to be played. Southampton's St. Mary's is a lovely stadium. All the new grounds are pretty much the same, but there is something special about this one. The home fans generate a decent atmosphere, and the view for the visitors is nothing short of first class.

We were the featured match on the following morning's Championship programme, and we all prayed that as league leaders, we wouldn't let ourselves down.

It didn't start well off the field. Danny Higginbotham was left out of the team as he awaited a move to Sunderland for £2.5 million. It left us even shorter in the centre of defence but we coped OK to begin with, and that man Fuller scored another cracker to put us ahead.

We were riding our luck. The Southampton fans continually boasted about the fact they hated local rivals Portsmouth. I don't care!

They had something to cheer about soon though, and they raced into a 3-1 lead after the break. We were being toppled from our spot at the summit.

The manager brought on his son, Anthony, and he managed to set up another goal for the Beast to make the score a little bit more respectable.

As we waited on the coach to leave, it appeared there were plenty of Southampton fans ready for a fight, and some drunk Stokies were ready for it too. Now Southampton are not a team I would associate with this sort of behaviour so it somewhat surprised me that they were there waiting.

The police were on hand to diffuse the situation, and we were off on our merry way….for four hours all the way back home!

"The lads prepare for battle at Southampton"

1 September 2007. Wolverhampton Wanderers (home)

The old Staffordshire derby returned, and it was a very poor match. The closest Stoke came in the first half was when a Wolves defender tried his luck and nearly rocketed a header in. Sadly it went just over.

One of the encouraging stories of the opening few weeks of the season was the return to fitness of Rory Delap. In just his second game last season he broke his leg against Sunderland (who he was on loan from). Stoke stood by him and went through with a permanent transfer as had previously been agreed with Sunderland boss Roy Keane.

The Irishman has done fantastically to get himself ready for this campaign, and has brought to the side an extremely dangerous weapon- his long throw. In the early matches of the season it took supporters by surprise- it must be the longest ever by a Stoke player.

It was Delap who was presented with the perfect opportunity to rid himself of the agonising memories of the previous season when he was put through on goal against Wolves.

As he rounded the keeper the vocal Boothen End rose as one ready to celebrate a last minute winner against our rivals but alas, he stumbled and failed to make further contact with the ball.

Aunty Isabelle was convinced he had been tripped. I stood to correct her, unless there was a rogue mole popping its head up from underneath the pitch!

The match ended in an unspectacular 0-0 draw.

15 September 2007. Hull City (away)

Rob and I boarded the coach in preparation for a tough fixture. We'd waited 2 weeks for this match. Apparently all football has to stop just because some overpaid internationals are kicking a ball about. Oh how I hate international weeks!

Due to a bit of aggro between these two sides at the end of last season, there were plenty of policemen on show in East Yorkshire. Due to Stoke fan's history of being, shall we say, slightly boisterous, all true supporters have to possess an ID card to gain entry to away fixtures.

This involves being treated like sheep- herded into the ground by stewards who have been specially shipped over from the Potteries. Clearly checking a piece of plastic is too much to ask for home stewards?

Hull was no different. We made our way in, settled down and read the programme with a re-heated beef and onion pie. This is football at its best.

It's a shame the action couldn't replicate our culinary delights. A decidedly average game turned on half time when Delap avoided the mole this time and struck his first goal for the club.

This prompted the most bizarre new chant of the season…"Über, Über, Über, Über" …German for super. Why this was sung I will never know. It was good fun though. The concourse was rocking. Quite literally! The shutters on the pie stands had been pulled down once the game re-started after half time but some lads who were just finishing their pints decided it would be fun to rattle them as loud as possible. The noise reverberated around the entire ground!

While all the Über chanting was going on, Hull brought on a fella by the name of Jay-Jay Okocha. He is officially 34, but it is believed, like a lot of African players, he is actually older than that. Whatever his age, he is a precocious talent. His appearance from the bench swung the game, and Hull salvaged a point from nowhere.

While on the coach waiting for departure, a load of Stokies decided to replicate a rugby ruck outside. The police charged in ready with their batons until they realised that perhaps they couldn't handle their drink and were just getting a bit overly pally!

Once the coach began rolling we were pelted by a little girl chav who decided she didn't want her Stella and it would be better to throw the can at the coach! She quickly scampered away once a copper began to walk towards her. Bless!

It was a real mission after the match. It was my aim to be back in Stratford by 8.30. Alexis had given me an ultimatum. I had to be back by that time to avoid going out clubbing! Under the thumb or what?! I made it with seconds to spare and settled down to watch Match of the Day. The perfect Saturday night!

"Twenty riot police…just a tad excessive don't you think?!"

18 September 2007. Barnsley (home)

A typical home night match against a supposed lesser side. Fairly cold, sparse attendance and awful atmosphere. Home matches aren't a patch on away fixtures. Our Britannia Stadium, despite being in place for ten years, will never replicate the history of the old Victoria Ground.

As much as the Brit is our home, most fans (if not all) would have preferred the old ground to be updated rather than demolished and left as wasteland for nine years. It is a great loss of a spiritual home.

On this particular Tuesday evening we were 'treated' to the Beast upfront. Sadly, he didn't grasp the opportunity in the same way that he had taken the bull by the horns when he arrived off the bench a couple of weeks ago. It was a poor performance not only by him, but the whole team.

At the previous ground there was an occasion when we beat Barnsley 5-4. What I would have given for just one goal tonight. This match was very poor and never really threatened to trouble the score line apart from one gilt-edged opportunity. Yorkshire man Cresswell had a ball put on a plate for him, but from 3 yards out he somehow put the ball over.

It summed it all up.

22 September 2007. Plymouth Argyle (home)

What a strange topsy-turvy game. Having left Stratford at 10.30, I had a bite to eat with Mum and Dad (tomato soup and a ham sarnie to be precise) before picking up my Aunty and heading off to the ground.

Sitting down with Dad and Aunty Isabelle, we browsed through the programme and much to our astonishment there was a two page feature on Rob. What a great way to start the afternoon!

Despite Plymouth being near us in the table, most fans turned up expecting a Stoke victory. All was going to plan. A Plymouth defender put the ball in his own net and all was going fairly swimmingly.

Well, swimmingly before we decided to turn extremely negative. Now, I am a huge fan of Tony Pulis. He performed a miracle in his first season in charge by keeping us up when we appeared to be dead and buried, and last year (in his first campaign back after a spell at Plymouth) he nearly took us into the play-offs.

However, he does at times have a tendency to be extremely defensive. In the second half we camped ourselves into our own half, invited pressure, and conceded two goals.

It was completely our own fault. We asked for it, and we got it. The fans turned. Screaming for blood. Pulis must go were the cries. Why are we defending so ridiculously against Plymouth? Plymouth I ask! Are they to be feared *that* much?

A trademark Delap throw saw wonder winger Lawrence bundle home a scarcely deserved equaliser which drew a muted response from the home fans. It was a strange celebration.

Having seemingly got out of jail (a little bit) Pulis really hit the jackpot. Ricardo Fuller, our influential striker, lobbed the ball past the Plymouth 'keeper to provide an almost embarrassing victory for us.

After the match Pulis decided to have a pop back at the fans, which did not go down well with the locals. He might have shot himself in the foot here- we have a wonderful chance of doing something this campaign but we all need to be singing from the same hymn sheet.

Look, we all make mistakes. Pulis made one by sitting a bit too deep and making un-timely comments. However, the main thing is we won. Hopefully we can all get on with it.

A big plus after the match was bumping into Andy and Chris. Andy is the editor of a website and asked me to get involved in writing the reserve team reports having seen me pop up on a messageboard. I was delighted to assist.

Despite only meeting him for the first time (I had seen his face knocking around for years) we chatted away for a good 20 minutes. That's the beauty about football. You can start talking to someone about it, and before you know, you've wasted half your afternoon!

Chris, his brother, surprised me. Shockingly I had met him in the past. Not at a Stoke match. Oh no. At Adelaide last year at the Australia v England second test. This was the ultimate in coincidences. I immediately recognised his face, although had spoken to him once in England- at Preston away last year at the bar. He piped up: "You got back OK from Australia then?!" Surreal stuff indeed!

So yeah, that was Andy and Chris. The website is quality. Andy knows what he's on about. It is just up to me to help him in any way I can. I might start writing some articles soon if he'll let me…. one thing at a time, calm down James.

"The legend that is James Knowles. Sorry, I mean Tony Pulis."

29 September 2007. Leicester City (away)

A massive occasion for me. Alexis' first ever football match. We had discussed it in the past and eventually it was the Walkers' Stadium that would provide her first 90 minutes of action.

We parked in a beautiful area of Leicester. On our quarter of an hour walk to the stadium we passed used mattresses, abandoned trolleys and old beer cans. Just a typical match day. To say Alexis was bemused would be a slight understatement!

I always get nervous before a match but today was a different feeling in my stomach. I was just praying that Stoke would do OK and the match would provide plenty of entertainment (or at least as much entertainment for a first timer as possible).

Stoke fans are fairly easy going when it comes to seats. It is an unwritten rule between us all that we just sit where we like. That's just how it is. As I was excited about the day (did I mention it was Alexis' first game?!) we got there well before kick off and sat down near the front to soak up some sun. A chief steward promptly ordered me to show him our tickets and then proceeded to point me in the direction of my seat. Bearing in mind there were about 100 Stoke fans in an area that held 2,000 supporters at this time, it seemed ludicrous that we were pointed to our seats- right next to a group of overweight lads.

Cramped up and sweating in the heat, we saw the fattest football fan of the season. A Leicester supporter was walking round the pitch topless and showing off his numerous tattoos related to his football club. Having trundled past the Stoke fans, he went into the stand and into his seat. He had an extra special seat- right at the top next to a drum. If there is anything more annoying at a football match than the drone of a drum going on for an hour and a half I am yet to hear it! The fat bastard chants were inevitable.

After the ridiculous situation involving the seats, two minutes before kick-off, the chief steward came up to his and declared we could sit anywhere. What a pointless exercise all that was!

So, after all this excitement, the football began and Stoke were doing well. Could we provide Alexis with a win on her debut? That man Fuller gave us a great start. Weaving inside and out of his marker he spanked the ball past the 'keeper to give us the lead inside 15 minutes. It came from nothing and really showed what a shining light Fuller is in our team. Alexis looked at me as though I was a madman, jumping around and lost in the moment. My reaction to the goal was nothing when compared to the man behind. He had clearly consumed too many pints and he fell over the chair onto Alexis' back. Welcome to a Stoke 'mental' darling!

As the fat man continued to bang his drum we held on until half time. However a masterstroke of a substitution from Gary Megson (who was working alongside Tony Pulis last month on a part-time basis) saw substitute Fryatt score 50 seconds after coming on. It was a kick in the teeth and after that there was never going to be a winner.

So, Alexis' first match. A 1-1 draw with the greatest excitement being a fat man with a drum. Not to worry, it's a start. She says she enjoyed it which is good enough for me even if she is only saying it to make me happy.

The next task is to drag her to another one.

3 October 2007. West Bromwich Albion (away)

With Dad away in Malta for a couple of days, Aunty Isabelle decided this would be a rare away day outing (in fact her last one was the corresponding fixture last season). We set off straight after I finished work and having searched for a place to park, ended up about 20 minutes away from the ground. Eating our onion laden cheese burgers along the way, we discussed our excellent record against the Baggies. We have only lost once at their place since 1988. Would that change tonight? I hope not.

West Brom are a very good side and we were a little bit worried about what might happen. Would our tremendous record count for anything? Every game is different.

John Eustace returned to the side in place of long throw man Delap. Eustace is a real fans' favourite. He has been at the club for four years but only played a handful of injuries due to a terrible injury record. Every time he puts on the red and white you fear it might be the last time. It really is that bad!

There was also a place on our bench for Vincent Pericard. Now Vince is an interesting figure. We sat next to him at last season's awards dinner and he hardly spoke a word. He is a very quiet chap. It was a bit of an eyebrow raiser then, when news broke that he had been locked up for four months for speeding and perverting the course of justice. Apart from this, Vince isn't even that good at football but fair play to Stoke for giving him a second chance.

On to the football. Shawcross gave us the lead with a well directed header and we were back at it again. Beating West Brom!

As I always do, I was taking a couple of photos of the match until an over eager steward raced up to me to clearly put me in my place and put my camera away.

Stoke were doing a superb job of wasting time here and there and slowing the game down. A victory against promotion rivals would be fantastic. Could we hold on? No. Despite only being 21 years old and a centre half, Leon Barnett managed to score his second career goal against us to draw WBA level. Twenty minutes of West Brom attacks resulted in nothing, and both teams had to settle for a point.

Once at home it was clear that West Brom were not happy. Comedian and Stoke fan Nick Hancock was incensed by what West Brom's local media were saying on the radio and decided to ring up to defend Stoke. We are not the most talented side in the world but Pulis has us playing to our strengths and does a fine job.

We went to the Hawthorns to get a point and we got it. It was up to West Brom to break us down and they couldn't sufficiently. It is their fault.

The next day's papers were full of praise for Stoke. Well, except the Midlands papers. The West Brom journalists would not stop blabbering on about how awful it would be to watch Stoke play each week. One journo compared it to a car crash and proclaimed he wouldn't pay money to watch it. I call it sour grapes personally and can't wait for the re-match at our place in December.

6 October 2007. Colchester United (home)

A home match against a struggling side points in all the wrong directions if you are a Stoke fan. We have a horrible habit of messing up in games we should win. A couple of years ago we managed to become the first team Rotherham had beaten away from home on a Saturday for a year. We tend to buck the trend when it comes to the poorer sides.

It was important that we didn't slip up here. Although unbeaten in six matches, we'd only won one of them and it was about time we got another three points on the board.

Again, the lads came out to a half empty stadium. With just over 12,000 present, it must be disheartening for the players to see so many red seats.

It is always important to start well in this type of game so the fans don't get a chance to get agitated and luckily we did. A powerful header from that man Shawcross put us ahead in the eighth minute in what could be described as the perfect start.

All was looking rosy until out of nowhere, Colchester pegged us back to send their handful of supporters into delirium.

It took us quarter of an hour to retake the lead and Lawrence did it, expertly finishing for his second goal of the season. Colchester's attack was rather powder puff from there on in and we held on for a well-deserved victory. A very important one too.

20 October 2007. Sheffield Wednesday (home)

The big one. Knowlesey v Gilley. Friendships are put aside and the real business is decided on the pitch. I'd gone to the trouble of ensuring with Aunty Isabelle that she wouldn't be at this match so Gilley could attend (as he has done for the previous five or six years). Sadly, last minute work commitments meant he would be in Shropshire at 3.00. This meant only one thing. Alexis' second match!

We have to win this. I can't lose to Wednesday- I will never hear the end of it! Fuller hadn't scored since that Leicester game and sure enough, he did the damage again. He used his pace to outmuscle the defence before coolly putting us one up. To say I was happy would be an understatement. This was more important than the average match!

Alexis said she was happy too. I think mainly because I get all grumpy when we lose! Excellent, we are beating Gilley's side. Just hold on lads and everything will be OK. Oh dear. Ten minutes later we are 2-1 down. How can this be happening? Aren't you listening? We can't lose this one Stoke!

Yes, yes, yes! Fuller has scored again. Perhaps he has a thing for my girlfriend? Alexis has been to two matches and he has scored three goals. Mmmm seems fishy! Nice one Ric, good finishing. It's 2-2 half time. Time to send Gilley a text. "We have the impetus mate, 2-2. Fuller on fire".

Wednesday's midfield comprised of Kavanagh (see Cardiff away) and an Irish lad called Glenn Whelan. Much to the potential anguish of Gilley, this week's rumour mill has linked Whelan with, amongst other clubs, Stoke,. I would love to see Gilley's face if we managed to prise him away from Hillsborough. Whelan is a quality midfielder and he performed very well in this game, running rings around our aging pair of midfielders.

I was feeling optimistic as we kicked off for the second period. We need to beat this lot. I don't think the lads are quite appreciating how important this one is. I kept receiving intermittent texts from Gilley. "What's the score mate?"…"Any more goals?". He left work at 4.30 and managed to listen to the final few minutes on the radio. As he was in Shropshire the reception was poor and all he could hear was the name Sweeney.

Peter Sweeney is a lad we signed from Millwall a couple of years ago but he broke his back in his first pre-season with the club and hasn't quite fulfilled his promise. Perhaps this could be his day? No. He messed around on the edge of his own area, gifted the ball to a Wednesday player and bang. They had retaken the lead. There are only five minutes left Stoke, at least salvage a draw!

No, Sweeney's at it again. 4-2. How embarrassing is this? Typically, Gilley had now picked up good reception on his radio and was basking in the glory. This is a sad day.

Sheffield Wednesday even had the cheek to bring on a former Port Vale striker, Akpo Sodje. Vale are our main enemy. They play just up the road in Burslem and as a result of their close proximity are the local rivals to Stoke City Football Club. Thankfully we are better than them but it would be nice to have some good old fashioned rivalry going on again. However, the way they are going at the moment that could well be a long cry away.

I could barely talk. Alexis tried to comfort me but there was nothing that could be done. I had lost to Gilley. Now I have to drive back to Stratford and pretend I'm mates with Gilley as though nothing has happened.

Nothing happened? Look at the scoreboard! At least we are above them in the table. Oh dear here we go…"Evening Gilley". That was about all I could muster all night.

Gutted.

"Mr Fuller knows who the main man is"

23 October 2007. Crystal Palace (away)

What kind of people do they employee at the fixture list organisation committee? To put us away at Palace on a Tuesday night is ludicrous. I barely managed a lie in. We left on the coach at midday for an 8.00PM kick off, trundling through Croydon at the worst possible hour. Absolute madness, it really was.

We'd already been travelling for a good couple of hours when we stopped at Oxford for an hour. Every single time we go on the coach the service station halts seem to get longer and longer. It is the one frustrating aspect. Luckily, Oxford has a good game station and Rob and I raced over to it (after a cheeky bit of crispy chicken). Showing off our football knowledge, we managed to bag ourselves a fiver. Thank you very much, that will pay for the programme. On to London we go.

Every coach journey sees the courier's come round and play a nice little football game. You pay 50p, pick a team and then a particular one is revealed. If you have the chosen team (out of the twenty available) you win a tenner. After the debacle against Sheffield Wednesday, I just had to choose them. Lo and behold, they were revealed and I had got £10. Easy stuff. That's my food paid for, plus change!

Having crawled through the London suburbs, we ended up at Selhurst Park. It is a horrible little ground. There is a supermarket shoved into one of the stands, and as an away fan you have a poxy little bar and pillars to obscure your view once in your seat.

Me, Dad and Rob decided to go right to the front so as not to have a pillar in our way. It was far from ideal but the best position in a bad situation. We were far from optimistic going into this one. Neil Warnock had just been appointed Palace boss and was making his first appearance in front of his home supporters. It always seems to happen in football, a new manager means a victory. That's just the way it is. Warnock is the kind of guy opposing fans love to hate. He has a decent track record as a manager but always gets up people's nose.

We may as well give it a go though. We don't want to turn up and roll over. Infact, we gave a decent account of ourselves first half. Mama Sidibe was out of action due to a horrendous ordeal. Whilst on international duty with Mali, angry Togo fans decided to invade the pitch and attack the successful Malian players. Sidibe was attacked with a belt and coins before being dragged through a window by his teammates to the relative safety of the dressing room. Needless to say, 'Big Mama' was severly shaken by the event and in tremendous pain. All this meant that Richard Cresswell was to play upfront for the first time in his Stoke career.

After an uncertain start to his time at Stoke, Cresswell hit the ground running in this one. Early in the second half he got on the end of captain Matteo's cross to put us 1-0 up. Fantastic! From nothing we have the lead. Keep it tight lads…

…What are you doing?! Dougie Freedman, who seems to have been around forever, tiptoes past Shawcross to equalise immediately. We didn't even manage to get our Delilah anthem in.

Great. We know what's going to happen now. We've read the script. Put us out of our misery Palace, get it over with. Hang on. Go on Lawrence, shoot lad! He hit the post but Cresswell was on hand to fire in his second of the night. Wow! 2-1 up. Well done lads. Just make sure you listen to me this time and keep it tight!

A typical Pulis side would defend in these situations. Soak up the pressure and hopefully hang on for all three points. Not tonight. We went for the jugular. Delap crashed a volley onto the underside of the crossbar before Shawcross came flying in and headed it onto the bar and over the line. The Beast was on hand to make sure and cheekily ran off claiming it was his. All this despite the fact it was about 3 yards over the chalk already!!

It all ended up being a comfortable victory for Stoke. Who would have predicted that one? Not me, that's for sure!

It makes the journey home so much faster and better when you are successful. It's still a bit painful arriving home at 2.30 in the morning knowing that in five hours you will be up again for work.

This is made even worse when you regret the moment you decided to write for the local paper, *The Sentinel* and log a 'fan's view' after every match. The last thing you want to do after a long day is scour your brain for intellectual thoughts on something you were watching five hours ago. Not to worry, a quick email and it's all done. 150 words, bish bash bosh, have that.

Bed time.

27 October 2007. Bristol City (away)

Dad very kindly detoured on his route from Eccleshall to Bristol, picking me up from Alexis' at about 11.00AM. As we always do, we discussed potential tactics and line ups. We are always wrong but we still do it every time. It's all part of the day.

We were in for a huge shock when we arrived at the ground though. Vincent Pericard was in the starting eleven. As mentioned before, Vince had some time in jail but was released early. However, 'problems with his tag' arose and he had to complete his stint. He came out of prison just three days before the Bristol trip. It seemed a strange choice but Pulis' hand was half dealt with the suspension of Cresswell and the injury to Sidibe.

Tony Pulis used to be a manager at Bristol City. He was an unpopular figure and received a chorus of boo's before kick off, which he took on the chin.

Ashton Gate is an unusual ground. It must be the only stadium in the country where there are portaloos outside the ground and the away end has seats with no backing to them, meaning you spend the whole match leaning forward and thinking you are about to fall over!

We had a couple of early chances, with Fuller going typically close but it was Bristol City who got the only goal of the game. Defensive midfielder Marvin Elliott had a shot which spooned over Simonsen and into the back of the net. It was extremely lucky but that's football.

Ten minutes later I noticed a number of high visibility jackets running into the top row of the stand to our right. I naturally thought it was a bit of trouble breaking out. I wish it was as it later transpired it was a relatively young gentleman dying of a heart attack. It puts things into perspective.

Rob (who is an avid *Only Fools & Horses* fan) pointed out that the tower block to our right was actually used for the exterior shots of Nelson Mandela House in the cult television series. A pointless fact that you probably never knew (or never needed to know!)

After slowly making our way out of the ground, despite the close attention of the police, we were greeted by home supporters throwing bottles and coins at us. Charming stuff indeed! Luckily, Dad and I had parked away from the official coaches so could make a quick exit. Or so we thought. As we tried to break away a policeman pulled me back and told me to go where everyone else was going. Am I a sheep? Why should I follow everybody else when my car is in the other direction? Thankfully the next policeman saw sense and allowed us to walk on to the vehicle. Bloody coppers at football- they don't understand!

Once home, I rang Rob to tell him of the incident. His was worse! As the supporters were shepherded towards the coaches they passed a 'home only' pub. The people in there then decided to let off fireworks and throw umbrellas around as though it's the new fashion. Sounds like mental stuff to me!

31 October 2007. Huddersfield Town (home, reserves)

My big break. Having already attended all reserve matches so far this season and writing for Andy's website, I took the liberty to contact *The Sentinel's* Sports Editor just to let him know I was available to write a report if they were ever in trouble.

Much to my astonishment his response was that the normal guy who does it has left and I can start reporting immediately. It was a perfect set of circumstances. I got the big one too. Huddersfield reserves at home. That's right, Huddersfield reserves at home. Jealous?!!

With my notepad and pen in hand, I jotted down every single incident. I didn't want to miss a thing.

Goal!! My first goal to professionally report on:

A flick-on from Parkin fed Vincent Pericard, who fired across the keeper for his second goal in as many games for the reserves.

There were more to come and the match ended 2-1 to Stoke. The score was academic. I was so excited to get my report across to *The Sentinel* HQ.

I raced home and typed away, carefully checking my jottings as I went along. Ever eager, I kept making errors so had to count to ten and get it all right. I emailed it across to the editor and sat back, waiting for tomorrow morning's paper to be released.

I could barely sleep, would it be OK? Sure enough, there it was in black and white with my name next to it. My report in the paper!! I'm so happy.

If only it was a few years ago. People could have been eating their fish and chips out of my report. Now that would be a scoop!

3 November 2007. Coventry City (home)

Having left it a bit late to leave Alexis, I was sweating a bit time-wise but I managed to make kick off and welcome our two new signings. As we are out of the transfer window, clubs can only make 'emergency loan signings', but everybody knew that Leon Cort and Danny Pugh were here for the long haul.

Neither of them made the best start to their Stoke careers. After an uneventful first half, where the only action was a minor skirmish between rival players, Coventry sprung into life in the second period.

The man they call the Maltese mosquito, Michael Mifsud, terrorised our new signing Cort and put them in the lead. Former Crewe man Dele Adebola then killed off the contest with his customary goal against Stoke. He shook off the attentions of Cort to double the lead.

Hang on! The referee has lost the plot. After waving away a blatant foul on Fuller in the area, he then points to the spot after a Coventry defender cleanly won the ball. Madness! Lawrence scores. 2-1 now, come on Stoke!

Bloody hell! Mifsud has scored again. It's definitely over now. Cort (who is rumoured to become our record signing) has had a nightmare, Pugh was anonymous and all in all, it has been a very bad day at the office.

On to the next match.

"Flexing the muscles for one last time before kick-off"

6 November 2007. Scunthorpe United (away)

Another new ground for me. Glanford Park is housed on a retail estate and is a pretty small stadium. The seats are practically on the pitch, leaving corner takers and long throw merchant Delap very little room to run up and master their arts.

In the summer, newly promoted Scunthorpe signed a young striker from Stoke, Martin Paterson. 'Patto' will sadly be remembered for missing an open goal against Cardiff last season when we were already 1-0 up. A win would have effectively sealed a play off place. We ended up drawing. However, he got a good reception and gave us a thumbs up when we all chanted "Patto is a Stokie", which was nice to see.

Scunthorpe started well but we took an undeserved lead through Cresswell. He poked the ball home at the far end to cue a delayed celebration from the supporters. We could barely see a thing and didn't have a clue who scored. We didn't care! 1-0 up.

The home side deservedly equalised, and Patto hit the bar. We were in trouble. We were sitting deeper and deeper which the fans were not impressed about. Some supporters were getting on Pulis' back, while others were appreciating the good job the home side were doing in pinning us back to our own area. The support was clearly divided.

Then came Pulis' masterstroke. With ten minutes to go, he took off right back Gabriel Zakuani and replaced him with fellow right back Stephen Wright. This defensive minded substitution drew a number of boos from the Stoke fans. Five minutes later we conceded. A bullet of a shot sparked scenes of frenzy. The home 'keeper raced to his own fans and slid along the ground as though he had won the World Cup.

Cue a large number of disgruntled Stokies getting up and leaving. I've never understood this leaving early business. You travel a couple of hours to a match, pay for your ticket and then miss 10% of it. Besides, you never know what could happen, that is why football is the greatest sport of all.

We've got a free kick. Just take your time. Composure Eustace, make it count. No! Don't pass to Wright, what are you doing? Wait a second. Yes!! Well done Eustace. Well done Wright. Well done Pulis. We've scored. From nowhere we have managed to get a goal.

Again, Cort and Pugh have been ragged, but the lads have dug them out of a hole and salvaged a point. Oh hang on, come on Pugh, get the ball in, we might grab a winner here. Almost in slow motion, the ball came in. Our weakest aerial player Lawrence rose to knock it past the 'keeper and complete the most remarkable ten minutes of football I have seen in my life.

Absolutely incredible.

10 November 2007. Sheffield United (home)

A late evening kick off to accommodate the SKY cameras meant an unusual 'warm up' to the game. I departed Stratford and listened to the commentary of the 3.00 kick offs on my way to the Britannia Stadium.

It won't be an easy game. Sheffield United were relegated last season and managed to spend £4 million on one player in the summer. Just to give all the clubs in the Championship a chance, they employed Bryan Robson, quite possibly the most overrated manager in England, to replace the departing Neil Warnock.

Alas, this one wasn't meant to be. We welcomed back Sidibe after his African horror and, sporting a cast on his arm, he played pretty well alongside Fuller.

It was Sheffield United loanee Gary Cahill who scored his second career goal against Stoke to condemn us to a third successive home defeat. If you are going to seriously challenge for promotion, you just cannot afford to lose that number of games on the trot- particularly on your own patch.

We now have to wait two weeks until our next game at Burnley. As England are playing, we have to endure McClaren's boring team on the box rather than being at 'proper' football.

Luckily next weekend is Alexis' birthday- a weekend that coincides with no Stoke match!! The pair of us, along with Gilley and Alana, are all going to celebrate in the hell hole that is Blackpool. It should be a good laugh. I think we will play a spot of pub golf which will be very entertaining- I just hope that everybody can handle the pace!!

24 November 2007. Burnley (away)

After the two week football absence, it was with great joy that we were at Turf Moor on this wet Saturday afternoon. Dad and I arrived nice and early, greeting the players off the coach. After a mild argument with Alexis, I needed to clear my head and football is generally the best place to do this. Well, except today.

Last season, high winds had meant that the visiting supporters were moved to a home area of the ground, but this year we returned to our rightful position. A large video screen had been placed in the away end, severely reducing the number of fans that could fit in (not that we sold out anyway).

Burnley is the only ground in the league that still has wooden seats. I can't say that I am particular happy about this. Not only does it break your back as they are so uncomfortable, it is also a bit of a health hazard, although the smoking ban has potentially reduced this threat.

The highlight of the day was seeing former Stoke favourite Vince Overson turn up in the Burnley youth development area of the ground. He got a standing ovation (any excuse to get off those wooden seats) from the Stoke fans, and he gave a polite wave before sitting down.

There was nothing to report on the pitch against a Burnley side who were being managed by Owen Coyle for the first time. This was after Steve Cotterill left the club a few weeks ago. Now, Cotterill is a hated figure at Stoke and has been given the nickname "Quitterill" by many Stokies. This was because, after only thirteen games in charge of us, he decided that it was much more attractive (sorry, lucrative) to become assistant manager at Sunderland. Much to the delight of the Stoke fans, his Sunderland side were relegated straight away.

So, no Cotterill to boo and no goals to cheer. A bore draw. Off to Cheltenham for a night out. Anything's better than that 90 minutes!

27 November 2007. Queens Park Rangers (home)

QPR and Stoke have a bit of history. Former Rangers player Marc Bircham got up everybody's nose after he wound up former defender Gerry Taggart a bit too much a few years back, and a Stoke fan put us on every news channel in the world when he ran on to the pitch and attacked their 'keeper. Why can't things just be quiet and normal? Perhaps tonight might just be different?

QPR have two 'managers' on their bench. One Italian coach, and his interpreter. What has English football come to? This can't be the correct way of doing things? An interpreter on the bench? What is the world coming to?!

We shut the pair of them up with a quick fire pair of goals. QPR had turned us round at kick off, so we were unusually attacking the Stoke core of fans in the Boothen End for the first 45. Cresswell scored from four millimetres before Lawrence curled a beauty of a free kick into the top corner. 2-0, surely job done?

Everything looked even better in the second half when their striker was shown a red card for a reckless lunge. We all sat back, ready for a goal glut. It didn't come, and we sat deeper and deeper. The lads behind me, Dad and Aunty Isabelle are fully against Pulis. What delight they took in our backs to the wall efforts. Screaming and balling at the manager, I must have had half a cup full of spit on my back. I buried my head in readiness for a waterfall when QPR pulled a deserved goal back.

Sadly for the lads behind, Leon Cort scored his first goal for the club to seal the points.

It wasn't vintage stuff but a win is a win.

1 December 2007. Norwich City (home)

A home match against a side in the bottom three should result in a victory, but Norwich are no mugs.

That said, I was expecting a victory. Former Stokie Darel Russell lined up for Norwich. With his vivid dreadlocks, he stands out like a sore thumb on the green grass- you can see him everywhere!!

A shoddy first half saw Norwich go into the interval 1-0 up, the little terror Huckerby scoring the goal. After the lacklustre performance, the lads came out with a renewed spirit and Leon Cort scored his second goal in as many games. Game on. Come on you Potters!

The attendance was swelled with a worthwhile local promotion from the club, and it looked like only a matter of time until we scored again. The fans who had made their way to the ground were determined to roar us onto victory. The atmosphere was electric. Fuller came close, as did Cresswell.

Just as it appeared that time was running out, a Lawrence corner fell to Cresswell who turned and powered home. A vital three points for us. We needed them. It keeps us in touch with the top.

Fingers crossed we can do the same at Sheffield United on Tuesday.

4 December 2007. Sheffield United (away)

After the Norwich match it was Alexis' Dad's works do. Tragically, Alexis' uncle died on the evening and everyone has been in shock ever since the event.

Football seems pointless after something so terrible happens in front of your eyes but I felt I just wanted to see my family so combined it with a trip to Bramall Lane (perhaps rather foolishly).

I was not particularly looking forward to the game. How could I? Nevertheless, Dad and I made the journey in somewhat sombre mood and arrived in Sheffield in good time. Picking up a hot dog (with customary tomato sauce and onions) we made our way into the away end, reading the programme as we squeezed through the turnstile.

I had barely eaten since Saturday, but the smell of all these pies and other calorie filled foods were too good to pass up so I indulged in another hot dog.

Despite only playing Sheffield United less than a month ago, we had the chance to gain revenge. Following that game, Bryan Robson compared us to the old Wimbledon side, which was far from complementary. I very much doubt that when he was in the Manchester United team they lost 3-0 at home to Wimbledon. However, that's exactly what we did to them. Three goals in the opening nineteen minutes secured the points. Firstly Cresswell kept up his good scoring record from two yards, before £4 million man Beattie headed into his own net and Shawcross netted a third.

It was surreal stuff. We were completely outplaying them. The Christmas songs came out, "Jingle Bells" and the like. I couldn't join in. I did afford myself a little smile though. 3-0 at Sheffield in their own back yard. This certainly doesn't happen every day.

We held on with minor scares for an extremely convincing victory.

Having stood all match (despite having perfectly adequate seats) we returned to the car and travelled home, listening to radio phone in programme 6-0-6 along the way, and hearing a text from Rob read out.

It was a match which to me never happened. There were other things going on.

God bless you Andy Campbell.

9 December 2007. Watford (home)

A late change to the fixture list to accommodate television demands meant this game fell on my birthday. Having been out very late the night before, my head wasn't quite ready to take in a football match. We stayed up all night watching the Ricky Hatton fight while naturally celebrating my birthday at the same time.

There wasn't much to get anyone overly excited in this one. Watford came to town top of the table but didn't do too much to suggest they were world beaters. In fact, we had the better chances. Fuller especially should have scored but he fluffed two glorious chances. He just needs one goal to get him going again. He is going through a lean spell.

Perhaps my earlier prediction that he had a thing for Alexis was wrong. She accompanied me to this match and the Jamaican didn't score. Perhaps it was a phase?!

The club had very kindly offered all season ticket holders a free ticket for this match (hence the fact Alexis was here). The PR is getting better by the day, and can only stand us in good stead if we were to reach the promised land that is the Premier League.

At least the new lads are beginning to settle in now. Cort has grabbed himself a couple of goals and now Danny Pugh (playing for the first time in the centre of midfield) has been named man of the match. Good stuff. Keep it up boys.

15 December 2007. Blackpool (away)

With Mum and Dad having departed to Australia for a month to see my sister in Adelaide, I dragged Alexis along to the Blackpool match. Bearing in mind she was off to Barbados for Christmas, I wanted to spend as much time with her as possible. If that involved the football, then brilliant!

For the first time at an away match, Rob and I were separated! Normally we buy tickets and then just sit wherever we like. Blackpool was different. We sold out our complete allocation and Alexis and I only just got our tickets! I was trying to rush through an ID card for Alexis to come to away games, but in the past I have managed to bring her along as a 'guest'. However, the guest list had been completely allocated and the card was cutting it very fine in coming through my letterbox. I bit the bullet and bought two tickets on the assumption the card would come in time. It did, but as it turned out nobody asked us to show them!

I started the afternoon by pigging out. Having found a nice American Italian restaurant, I dragged Alexis along and chomped away on potato skins and pizza. Only the healthy option for me! Alexis was eating a salad. I just don't do greens!

We trundled our way to the ground and into our temporary accommodation. The stand the Stokies were housed in was borrowed from the UK Golf Open. Now, stands for golf fans and football fans should be completely different. As far as I'm aware, golf fans don't jump around like lunatics if Tiger Woods holes a putt.

Anyway, we got to our seat but ended up standing for the entire game. With no roof, it was difficult to generate any kind of atmosphere. It was as though the songs were divided into three sections: right side, centre, left side. We were looking OK but it was difficult to play football. With an open end, the wind made life tough and it was Blackpool who took the lead against the run of play.

With so many away fans there, it made it feel a bit like a home match (although I don't think I'd like to watch every other game from a temporary stand). Having fluffed a few chances before, Fuller got back to his scoring ways and rifled in an equaliser before Cort got the stand rocking with a strong header.

Literally rocking. One bloke got so excited he made a hole in the stand which did not seem too safe. To have a stand of such atrocious quality should not be allowed in football- not just at this level, but at any. In fact, in the second half, a steward was ordered to stand over the hole so nobody fell through!

A second goal from Fuller right in front of us ensured the game was ours. Goals are a bit like buses aren't they Ric? You wait two months for one and then you get two!

A late consolation goal from the Seasiders left us sweating a bit but the result was never really in doubt.

All that was left to do, was to pick up a customary piece of rock and head off home.

"The hole"

22 December 2007. West Bromwich Albion (home)

Every once in a blue moon you get the perfect match. This was it. Sadly, everyone had gone away for their Christmas festivities so just myself and Aunty Isabelle were able to witness it. To say we enjoyed it would be an understatement.

After our battling draw at the Hawthorns and the negative press towards our approach that night, we wanted to show West Brom our real football.

An exquisite flick from Sidibe put Fuller through on goal and we had an early lead. The perfect start, just so long as we don't sit back and defend for 85 minutes! WBA came back at us. We were under an immense spell of pressure from the Midlanders. We just had to beat them after their comments earlier in the campaign. Besides, as we were singing, we always beat West Brom.

Against the run of play, Fuller grabbed a second. The perfect moment, just before half time too.

Then came the coup de grâce. Attacking the Boothen End, Ricardo Fuller picked up the ball on the half way line and raced towards goal. As one, the whole stand rose slowly as Fuller edged ever nearer to the net. Beating his marker, he coolly slotted past Kiely to complete a quite remarkable hat-trick. This is it. Who needs drugs? Football is my drug. A complete release of tension as victory is surely complete. Against the league leaders too. Absolutely magnificent!

There was still time for West Brom to pull a soft goal back, and for Leon Cort to dice with death and nearly present them with another one but this was one of those days when everything was perfect.

With me and Aunty Isabelle still buzzing, we queued for some tickets for the forthcoming away fixtures and waited patiently on the car park. The car park at Stoke is quite possibly the worst in the country. It is a free for all with cars coming at you from all angles, trying to get out as soon as possible. On this occasion we sat back, put on the local radio and smiled.

Perfection, absolute perfection. What a Christmas present.

26 December 2007. Barnsley (away)

Boxing Day- a day for hangovers, full bellies and football! Quite often the game after Christmas Day proves to be dull and lethargic. This was an exception to the rule.

Rob and I managed to sit next to each other again, and Rob's mate Rich joined us. The day in the ground didn't start off too well. I bought a programme and put it under my seat (as I always do) and went for a quick chat with a mate. I returned to find it had been stolen! Why would someone steal a programme? Despite looking like an idiot chatting away to stewards for half an hour, I ended up admitting defeat and bought my second programme of the day. Not good!

The match didn't have the greatest start either. What looked like a soft penalty was given to Barnsley at the far end and the resultant spot kick was confidently rolled home.

Having scored five goals in two games, it is fair to say that Fuller is in a bit of form. His electric pace terrorised Barnsley all afternoon and one particular run saw him theatrically fall to the ground to win the second penalty of the day. Lawrence scored, and we were back to square one.

With Sidibe still chasing his elusive first goal of the season, the striker tried his best but continually failed miserably. We were made to pay for our missed chances as Simonsen made a pig's ear of a routine cross and Macken scrambled the ball home.

As time marched on and into the final six minutes of normal time, our only hope was that substitute Parkin would salvage something. No, a superbly worked free kick routine ended up with Lawrence firing home for the equaliser.

Just as we all rose to sing Delilah, a cross from the Barnsley right wing was again spilled by the usually immaculate Simonsen into the path of Macken. All the hard work had been undone.

It was a real kick in the teeth. To come back and have it snatched away was hard to take. Now I know how Scunthorpe felt a few weeks ago. As the fourth official came out with his little electronic board and signalled four minutes of additional time, there was a glimour of hope that we might just have one more sniff. Somehow, after a Barnsley defender was sent off, the referee saw something in the area (possibly someone breathing on Parkin?) and pointed to the spot. Here was our chance to grab something. Rich looked away while we stared at that white ball, willing it to hit the back of the net. As the clock ticked over to 98 minutes played, Lawrence struck it, and as we had wished, the ball hit the net. Goal!!! A second consecutive hat-trick for Stoke and a load of Stokies going bonkers. Hangovers? What hangovers?

The draw felt like a victory. Another topsy-turvy final ten minutes. This kind of football is not good for my health!

29 December 2007. Plymouth Argyle (away)

I went to bed on the Friday prepared for an early start the next morning. The coaches were due to leave at 8.00AM so I set my alarm for 6.00, with the intention to put it on snooze a couple times. As I heard my phone go off I naturally assumed it was my alarm. To my shock it was 7.58 and it was Rob asking where I was. Somehow my alarm had let me down. This is what happens when there is nobody to wake you up!!

After a few swear words we agreed that we would (hopefully) meet at Hilton Park service station, some thirty miles away from the Britannia Stadium. In a race against time, I quickly woke myself up, put on a quick burst of deodorant and rapidly brushed my teeth. Constantly looking at my watch, I double checked my ticket was in my wallet and jumped into the car.

I was adamant I was behind the coaches and kept in constant contact with Rob. The last thing I wanted to do was drive all the way down to Plymouth. Screaming down the motorway, I made into the services and much to my astonishment there were no coaches there. I had beaten them! The next task was to pay for all day parking. For God's sake! The machine isn't working!! Running inside the service station, I barged through the queue of Blackpool supporters (who were travelling to Colchester) and pleaded with the woman behind the counter to issue me a parking ticket. She obliged.

By the time I affixed my ticket, the coaches had arrived, and much to the amusement of everybody on board, I walked on, together with my red face!

A stroke of luck that I made it then- this game better be worth it! After such an eventful start, the journey down was much quicker than it usually is to Plymouth. Rob had saved me a seat and we spent most of the time messing around on my Playstation Portable- anything to pass the time on these journeys!

Every club has them and we are no different. The one supporter who is a bit 'special' and different to everyone else. Rob and I have christened him 'Smiler'. Smiler doesn't really say much, he just makes weird noises at inappropriate times. He's a weird one and a bit of a fruitcake. As we wandered around (another) service station, he began talking rubbish to us. In the process he managed to knock over a stand of DVDs, much to our amusement. Always good value for some kind of a laugh is Smiler.

Having arrived at the ground ridiculously early, we had a couple of walks round the ground, sampling the portakabin they call the club shop along the way.

Last season the Plymouth stewards were overly forceful in their way of handling a few Stokies who were standing up while enjoying the game. On our entrance this year, we were informed that there was strictly no standing. We had been warned! The last thing I wanted to do after the earlier fiasco was to be thrown out of the ground!

Whilst in Plymouth it would be rude not to eat a pasty- they are from here so they must be good. My Cornish special was spot on and filled me up beautifully, together with my Bovril.

After his catastrophic afternoon at Barnsley, Simmo was dropped for the first time in 108 league games to be replaced by Hoult. It was a bold decision from Pulis. Would it work? We will find out in a couple of hours.

We were all on our feet early on as Fuller collided with the post and Cresswell knocked the ball in. A super start for us. A large number of young Plymouth fans (with an average age of twelve) were giving verbals to the 700 or so Stokies, mainly made up of grown men. Those little 'uns have balls of steel these days!

Disaster struck on the stroke of half time. Shawcross went in for a tackle and handled the ball as he did so. Penalty. Hoult (making his league debut) guessed the right way, making a tremendous save, only for the rebound to be smashed home for an equaliser.

There was only one thing that could be done. Shawcross had to redeem himself. Rising highest from a corner, he headed home. Yes! Back in the lead. As there were some spare seats next to us, I celebrated by running the length of the row and back again. I'm knackered! I don't care though, we have scored. A goal is a strange feeling. Sometimes you can play a whole game and not score once- it is a major event. A week's frustration is released in that one moment. You are lost. Nothing in the world matters apart from that leather ball hitting the back of the net.

Ten minutes later, Hoult was rooted to his line and they equalised. Get out there and punch it Hoult! Some open play followed and the game was up for grabs for either side. Plymouth's moment came. Ebanks-Blake forced Hoult out of his goal and out of his area. As he rounded the keeper, Hoult cynically chopped him down and was walking before the red card was produced for Stoke's first sending off of the season. So, Simmo was back in goal (at the expense of substitute Parkin). What an ironic end to the match it was. An athletic save by Simmo denied Ebanks-Blake (legitimately) and we escaped with a point.

"The man of the moment, Liam Lawrence"

1 January 2008. Hull City (home)

A New Year and hope for what may happen in 2008. We can only pray that it is better than this.

Having celebrated the New Year with some mates in Stratford, without any sleep I decided to get up to Eccleshall as soon as I could. Having made myself a bowl of pasta, I picked up Aunty Isabelle and we got to the ground.

It truly was a terrible game. The only high point was that we avoided defeat. A long throw from Delap was met by the head of Leon Cort, who scored against one of his old clubs. It is truly astonishing how many times a player comes back to haunt his old employees. That's four goals already for the defender, with surely more to come. What a signing this lad is turning out to be after his shaky start.

The average football continued and Hull got a deserved equaliser to ensure the spoils were shared.

The talk was that if we play like that against Newcastle, we will be absolutely hammered. Let us wait and see.

6 January 2008. Newcastle United (home)

Alexis has arrived home from Barbados. Delighted to see her, I gave my ticket away for Aston Villa v Man Utd to our neighbour, and rushed down to Stratford to greet her. It seems like a lifetime ago since we last hugged. Extortianate phone rates has meant talking has been limited in the past couple of weeks. Luckily, Stoke's massive cup tie has been put back 24 hours to a Sunday kick off, meaning I can spend a fair amount of time with Alexis.

The FA Cup third round is one of those special days in the football calendar. These days, because of the heightened media interest in football, the ties take place over two days, with the major matches generally taking place on Sunday for telelvision coverage. With Stoke riding high and Newcastle struggling in the Premier League this was seen as a prime choice to see an upset. Yesterday's fixtures saw Everton dumped out of the cup by lowly Oldham. Could we do the same?

There was a tremendous buzz around the club in the week leading up to the match. Management and players were constantly on the television being asked their opinions on the match. The club had organised a special entrance for the players as they walked out of the tunnel. We weren't left disappointed. The Seddon Stand (facing the camera) held aloft red and white cards to depict our club stripes, and fireworks were set off. It was like being at an El Clásico in Madrid!

Despite the game being televised on BBC, our biggest attendance of the season (22,861) was at the Britannia. This just shows the potential support for the club if we were to get promotion. The global side of English football was evident. My Dad was watching in his hotel room in Singapore (at 2.00AM) while my cousin, Mike, was viewing in New York. It really is incredible how far football has come in the last fifteen years.

England international Michael Owen started upfront for Newcastle. We have never had a player of his calibre at the Britannia. This is the type of star we want to see down here every week next season. Our defence kept him fairly quiet throughout and with a vociferous crowd, we held on until half time.

All pretty easy this is. Sam Allardyce, their manager, is under extreme pressure and a Stoke win would surely see him out of a job by the next morning. Big man Parkin came on to replace Sidibe on the hour mark and nearly sent us into wonderland immediately.

Within 20 seconds of coming on, Fuller went on a merry dance round the Newcastle defence and pulled the ball back into the path of the Beast. All he has to do is hit the target. He has, we have scored! No. Somehow, defender Faye blocked the ball and it agonizingly rolled away for a corner. Our big chance had gone. Despite other opportunities, it really was the Parkin chance which will be remembered. It was a game we could so easily have won. We restricted the Premier League 'giants' to very few sniffs at goal, with young full backs Andy Wilkinson and Carl Dickinson doing a sterling job on the Newcastle wingers.

Before the draw for the third round was made, my dream tie was Newcastle away. My wish was (half) granted as we held on for a draw, and a replay at St James' Park.

It was a day to be proud to be a Stokie. We gave a really good account of ourselves, and received the accolade of the local and national media the next day. Just imagine what it would have been like if we had won?!

"An incredible scene at kick-off"

12 January 2008. Ipswich Town (away)

Having endured such a long period of time without Alexis, I decided to drag her along to this one. After an energy sapping drive across the A14 from Stratford, we arrived in Ipswich at the exact same time as the official coaches. We saw Rob clamber off his coach so ran over to him to get his attention. Fully kitted out in Stoke colours, we headed into town looking for a 'safe' pub. Having found a relatively safe one, we sat down and I tucked into my juicy lamb burger with side salad. It was all a bit different from a mince pie or sausage roll.

Portman Road holds good memories for me. I hold an undefeated record here, and was hoping for it to continue. Today would be tougher than other encounters though. Jim Magilton has somehow moulded his side undefeated at home. In January? This is some record! Could we burst the bubble? With the replay at Newcastle looming, it is quite possible our minds would be elsewhere, but we will give it a go.

Outside the stadium there was some mad-man with a loud speaker 'singing' Ipswich related songs. There he was, walking up and down the road, all on his own, singing songs off the top of his head. You had to pity the guy. One Town fan came up to me and said, "Every club has one, and there's ours. The village idiot!" He summed it up perfectly.

It was a disappointing start to the game. A mistake by Dickinson allowed Ipswich to take the lead, and another hero of the Newcastle game, Wilkinson was withdrawn early on due to injury. It was a blow to the system and Wilko's replacement Zakuani was looking shaky. Surely our terrific unbeaten run was coming to an end?

Just hold fire. Stoke aren't dead until it's all over. A bit of magic from Fuller levelled things up. A superb piece of play on the left wing, culminated in a quality finish. All square, and all to play for.

The previously shaky Zakuani was beginning to step up to the mark, and he made a world-class challenge to prevent a certain Ipswich goal. That tackle effectively signalled the end of the game and with little more attacking play we came away with a fully deserved, and welcome point.

All that was left was to drive the long journey back to Birmingham for a trade exhibition the next day. Fun certainly isn't the word. Dressed up in a suit (I don't do suits) I felt like a right wally.

Hey ho, at least this weekend brought up another point on our league tally and continue that unbeaten run to twelve, although there have been too many draws in recent weeks.

16 January 2008. Newcastle United (away)

So, again we come up against the Premier League side. Perhaps we had thrown away our chance at the Britannia Stadium ten days ago? Nevertheless, there were 3,000 optimistic Stokies who made the journey up to Newcastle to roar on the lads. A normal league match will see two or maybe three official coaches taking supporters. On this occasion there was a mind blowing seventeen coaches!

Due to the late announcement of ticket releases, Rob had to queue up on my behalf to get a couple of tickets for me and Dad. It was a manic day when the news broke that tickets were on sale! No worries, Rob succeeded in the scramble and we boarded coach one, about seven hours prior to kick off. As I like to keep things nice and busy, I decided to work in the morning and then drive straight to the Brit to catch the coach.

The journey up to Tyneside was a bit different. We had an entire re-run of the first game against Newcastle AND the Ipswich match. I could have thought of better things to watch! As we approached Derby, the couriers came round with their little 'guess the team' game. Dad appropriately chose Derby County, and bagged himself a tenner in the process.

I mentioned that in the previous game 'Big Sam' Allardyce was under pressure. It in fact turned out to be his last game and after the Geordies were thumped 6-0 at the weekend, we believed we did have a glimmer of a hope of an upset.

Half way through the journey, Steve, Rob's brother, turned to us with some 'breaking news'. Kevin Keegan has just been announced as the new Newcastle manager. It was a complete bolt out of the blue. We quickly spread the word round the coach, before thinking (after about fifteen minutes) it could have been a wind-up. Frantically checking the internet on our phones (technology these days is fantastic) we couldn't find any news! We'd been had!

Laughing at the prank, we were stopped by Sue (who is a fellow fan's view columnist in *The Sentinel*) who had received news that it had been confirmed. This news virtually killed any chance we had of causing an upset. The place would be rocking. Keegan is a hero up there and they will be delighted. It soon became apparent that they were indeed delighted, and there were huge queues at St James' Park for tickets to the night's match.

Having been on the coach for a good few hours, we eventually arrived at our service station, which happened to be at Washington. We played Sunderland last year and took one coach plus a mini-bus and this service station was fairly cramped then. You can imagine the squeeze when seventeen coaches of Stokies converged on the place!

Needless to say, the services just couldn't cope. With a 7.45 PM kick off, we wanted to get off as soon as possible. With time marching on, I asked a copper what time we would be departing. "Half six, and no earlier", he told me sharply. Questioning why so late, he said that it is normal policy and that any idea of a delayed kick off (due to the late demand for tickets in the home end) is out of the question, Newcastle simply "never delay kick-off".

Much to our pleasure, the policeman was wrong. Once we were moving again, Barry (the driver) tuned into the local radio, and it was announced kick-off had been put back by quarter of an hour. We could breathe a little easier now.

Upon arrival (following a nice detour through the city and past the Angel of the North) we realised it was quite a walk to the away section. Fifteen flights of stairs to be precise. This was my first visit to the stadium and I have to admit I was very impressed with St James' Park. It is a monumental building. The main problem though, was that we were housed somewhere in the clouds (quarter of a mile away from the far corner flag!). The players on the pitch looked ants. It was almost like a game of Subbuteo was going on below us!

We couldn't really make out who the players were out there but we were well aware how close we were to taking the lead. A double chance went begging in the second minute and we were left to rue it.

A few minutes later, the (doubly) tiny Owen somehow sneaked in behind our defence to put the Geordies in to the lead. With very little segregation between home and away fans, this could have easily led to trouble. All there was between the sets of supporters was a thin line of stewards. Strangely, all the Newcastle supporters to our left looked under 16. It was a bizarre sight- not one adult at all, but thankfully there was no trouble.

After a horror tackle from a little scamp called Emre on Eustace earned him a red card, we were given renewed hope. For 60 seconds that is. A corner was headed home, and at 2-0 down it was all but over. The home supporters rejoiced in the fact 'King Kev' was returning home, and our performance was one of the weaker of the season, eventually resulting in us falling four goals down.

So, our day out had been ruined, but at least former Sunderland winger Lawrence scored the best goal of the match. It was scant consolation. The goal sparked a singsong from the travelling Stokies, a happy 50th birthday chant to Tony Pulis.

It wasn't the best way for him to celebrate.

"Dad being pointed in the right direction…don't look down!!"

19 January 2008. Preston North End (home)

After the excitement of the FA Cup, it was back to the bread and butter of the league. This really was a game we had to win. It's nearly a month since our last victory (six games ago) and we needed to get back on the rails.

Preston are languishing at the wrong end of the table, but last season were on the edge of the play-off positions so this was no foregone conclusion. With us boasting two former Preston heroes in our line up (Fuller and Cresswell) it is fair to say that Preston fans wanted to show them that they made a mistake in leaving Deepdale.

It was our new permanent signing that opened the scoring though. Twenty-nine years after Trevor Francis English football's first £1 million player, Stoke broke the barrier for the first time. Leon Cort put pen to paper on a £1.2 million deal from Palace, after a successful loan spell. He celebrated by nodding in a long throw from Delap.

Before half-time, almost embarrassingly, Cresswell made it 2-0. A cross from new signing Andy Griffin was inexplicably dropped by the Preston keeper and Cresswell tapped home.

The story of Griffin is quite interesting. Although born in Wigan, he came through the ranks at Stoke, making his debut as a seventeen year old in 1996. After impressing at Stoke, he was signed for a hefty fee of £1.5 million by Newcastle, and, after scoring against the mighty Juventus in the Champions League, he was snapped up by Portsmouth. It never quite worked for him on the south coast, and last season he came back to Stoke for two separate loan spells. During these spells he scored two cracking goals. One came in the 4-0 demolition of Leeds, and another in thick fog against Coventry. He was all set to sign permanently for us in the summer, but decided instead to join newly promoted Derby, much to the displeasure of most Stokies. He clearly saw sense though, and has now rejoined the club he started out with, for his fourth spell (the only player in our history to have done so)!!

With everything looking rosy, three points were surely in the bag. It isn't Stoke without making us sweat though. It was a former Stoke youngster who came to haunt us. Back in 2002, Lewis Neal supplied a crucial cross for Ade Akinbiyi to head home a goal that kept us in our current division. This time, in the white of a Preston strip, he nodded back for his team-mate Brown to stab home and make us all sweat.

Thankfully, we weren't sweating for too long. Within four minutes Cort had already nearly justified his expensive move and had scored his second. His header was adjudged to have crossed the line to send us home happy.

A very necessary three points had been chalked up.

23 January 2008. Leicester City reserves (away)

In line with my reserve match reports for *The Sentinel,* Dad and I travelled to Hinckley United (along with a dodgy sat nav) to see the second string up against Leicester.

It was a relatively ordinary game, which Leicester won 2-1, thanks to a screamer from their little midfielder after The Beast had rolled home a penalty for us.

It was soon clear that Stoke were fielding two trialists in their line-up. Being the journalist that I wish to be, I took it upon myself to find out. Having been unsuccessful in finding out the identities from Tony Pulis and reserve team manager Mark O'Connor, my only hope was to speak to the lads in person.

I caught the striker as he was warming down. He was only too happy to effectively tell me his life story. This was my first exclusive scoop! OK, although not very big, I was happy enough at finding out. He was a Dutchman of the name Johan Pater who was previously on the books of PSV Eindhoven, playing alongside the likes of van Nistelrooy and van Bommel.

Following his father's death, he now finds himself in the second division in Holland, and had been invited to Stoke for a couple of days. His performance was hardly going to earn him a contract but at least I had found out his name for my report. Accordingly, his name was in the paper the next day.

I was happy with my day's work. I had found out his name, and our goalkeeper's (Austrian, Robert Almer) and had submitted my report. What did strike me as odd was that having spoken to a number of contracted Stoke City players who were involved, none of them knew the names of these trialists. It must be rather difficult playing with players who you don't even know the names of!

A couple of days later some news broke from Holland. Pater wasn't meant to be in England. He had officially gone AWOL and I was the one who broke the news! I felt pretty bad to say the least, especially when I heard that he had been sacked by his club.

All I was doing was my job, what else should I have done? Oops, I don't think this was meant to happen!
Thankfully, Pater has now found a new club, and ironically scored his first goal for them against the club that sacked him.

All's well that ends well!

"The man they call Johan Pater"

29 January 2008. Charlton Athletic (away)

A long journey down to the capital to visit another new ground (this tally is ever increasing!) We were 'blessed' to have an incompetent driver on our travels. Regular driver Barry had been replaced, and as soon as we approached The Valley it was clear that the substitute was not up to it! Instead of heading to the ground we went in completely the wrong direction and had a lovely tour of the Millennium Dome. This was all well and good, but not 45 minutes before kick-off.

We had been delayed due to horrendous traffic problems and were beginning to wonder whether we would make kick-off. After our 'tour', we circled a roundabout and were then dumped on a dual carriageway, about half a mile away from the ground. It wasn't the best start possible!

Having walked to the ground, we were guided to the away end by a lovely sarcastic copper. The Valley's away end is of the older generation. The bar is in the open air and there is a two-tier set of seats. Stoke only had a smattering of fans in the lower tier. A Tuesday night in London is hardly going to entice many along. One of the people in the Stoke end was Portsmouth defender Linvoy Primus, seemingly there to see his old mate Salif Diao (who didn't even get on the pitch all evening).

We came to London with the intention to grab a draw and nothing more. It wasn't very pretty and our time wasting was at times unnecessary. However, I am willing to back the manager's judgement, but it sadly back-fired.

A late goal undid our defensive work, with a headed goal from Lloyd Sam, the smallest man on the pitch, although the build-up looked decidedly close to being off-side. Substitute Parkin nearly scored, but a marvellous save from Weaver denied him.

It was while on the coach, in a traffic-jam waiting to get out of London, when Rob turned to me and suggested the idea of this book. Thanks Rob, you have made me spend way too much time compiling this book, it's all your fault mate.

The journey back was almost as fun as the journey there. Clipping kerbs, going in the wrong direction- it's all part of the fun travelling to away matches!

So, our first league defeat since November 10th. It had to come at some time, and it came against our promotion rivals. Let's get back on track on Saturday lads.

31st January 2008. Deadline day.

This following piece was an article I wrote for The Sentinel at midnight, at the turn of the month. The crazy people at the Football Association decided a couple of years ago that clubs could only buy new players in the summer (up until the end of August) and the month of January.

The previous deadline day (on the final day of August) saw us patiently waiting for a star name. Alas, it appeared it was on its way. At 6.00 PM, Chairman Peter Coates announced an international player was due to sign imminently. Sadly, that player turned out to be Demar Phillips. He has since managed just 86 minutes of first team action. After that fiasco, we weren't expecting much this time around!

It is a truly bizarre situation, but one that clubs must adhere to. The 31st January was spent scouring the internet for rumours and new signings across the country. I found most of my day was spent on the renowned Oatcake message board. The Oatcake is one of the best fanzine's in the country, and its message board, one of the busiest. Full of Stokies posting rubbish. "My Gran saw Pele down the ground with his boots in hand". You know, the usual crap!

Well, that's another transfer deadline day over. What a busy one.

We had to wait for the action to come our way and to be perfectly honest, I think most Stokies expected nothing to happen.

Instead, we sold our captain to a promotion rival. On the face of it, this sounds silly business. In my eyes it is a decent deal for Stoke. The popular character had seen his better days before his horrendous injuries, and despite being a regular starter for us in recent weeks, most fans could see he wasn't the player we once knew and loved.

Eustace will go down as a bit of a legend at the Britannia Stadium (despite only making 71 appearances) and all fans will wish him the very best for his career at Watford. We just hope for his sake that he doesn't suffer any more career threatening injuries.

So, the question on everybody's lips was "who is the replacement?" Surely the hierarchy wouldn't let him go without having someone lined up? Sure enough, in comes the popular figure of Paul Gallagher. His first spell at Stoke under Boskamp was a huge success and there were many supporters disappointed when he decided to join Preston on loan at the end of the last transfer window.

The reason he joined Preston was because we wanted to have him in a left wing role and Mark Hughes was only willing to allow his release if he was to be deployed upfront. Perhaps he has had a change of heart, as, despite his tremendous attitude, Cresswell is simply not a winger, and Pugh is better in a left back role.

The next thing to be decided is who will take the armband? In my eyes it will more than likely be Leon Cort who has been handed the armband when Eustace has been substituted in recent weeks. Andy Griffin will also be a contender, especially as he has recently signed on a long term deal.

The third option could well be Glenn Whelan. We had to wait until 11.34PM to hear of his £500,000 transfer from Sheffield Wednesday but what a tremendous signing. In my eyes he is twice the player of Eustace, and is a shrewd bit of business by Pulis.

After the heartache of the Charlton match it was clear to see that some new blood was required. The managerial team have responded well by bringing in both Gallagher and Whelan and we just hope that they can have a positive impact on the team and lead us to the ultimate goal. Promotion.

It was worth staying up until midnight! Whelan has joined. Cue the inevitable text from Gilley: "Without Whelan we will go down. I have never felt so gutted in my life". At least for his sake Wednesday signed Kavanagh on a permanent basis.

It was scant consolation for him.

2 February 2008. Cardiff City (home)

It's those fella's from Wales again, this time on our own patch. Having snatched the win on the opening day, Cardiff went on a terrible run, but are now considered the form team in the division and are on the edge of the play-offs.

Our line up saw Whelan and Gallagher start on the bench, with Salif Diao making his first start since re-signing for the club. Diao had a cracking time at the Brit last season. He initially joined us on loan from Liverpool (having commanded a fee of £5 million to move to Anfield) before completing a permanent short term deal.

Lack of fitness over the summer saw him hold off signing for anyone, and it looked increasingly likely that when he did sign for a club, it wouldn't be us. However, at the start of December, he penned a deal but niggling injuries have seen him wait two months for his first start.

The kick-off to the match had been moved to 12.30 due to concerns from the Staffordshire police that trouble may well occur. So, an early start and neither side seemed awake for the opening half. In fact, it was a Cardiff player who gave us the lead. Roger Johnson didn't know how to deal with a Lawrence corner, and he scored his second own goal in a week. Get in!

Hit-man Fuller was showing a great turn of pace and trickery against the Cardiff defence, and a gliding run resulted in him being scythed down by a defender. The only decision for the referee was to decide what colour card to give the lad, the penalty was obvious. Having chosen yellow, Fuller sent the keeper the wrong way to put us two up.

It was all looking good, songs reverberated around a surprisingly sunny Britannia Stadium. That was until former Chelsea striker Jimmy-Floyd Hasselbaink decided to score a goal, and it was only due to a wonderful save from Simonsen that he didn't score on a second occasion. I told you Stoke don't do things easily!

Despite strong pressure, we were able to give Whelan his debut which stabilised the ship. His calming influence saw us to a deserved three points over the ninety minutes.

Oh Gilley, what are you going to do without Glenn? To see him in red and white, not blue and white, must really hurt you. I'm sorry mate.

The aftermath of the Cardiff match saw me receive a phonecall from a withheld number and it turned out to be Setanta Sports. Earlier in the season I had agreed to be one of the Stoke fans on their database but hadn't heard anything back from them since. This lady wanted me to have a chat with Steve Claridge live on TV. How very exciting!

I frantically texted as many people as I could- "I'm on TV in half an hour!!" Rob replied with a little task: Get the word 'Stein' in the conversation. Mark Stein is an absolute legend at Stoke. He fired in the goals to take us up into Division One in my first season as a supporter, and is affectionately known as 'The Golden One'. I duly got his name in, much to the delight of Rob, and the bemusement of Claridge!

Two days after, Rob received a phone call from Radio 5 Live in relation to an incident between Cardiff boss Dave Jones and the ballboys. Jones didn't like the slow use of the multi-ball system and duly had a go at one of the youngsters. Needless to say, this didn't go down well with the Stokies who threw a barrage of abuse Jones' way.

A similar thing happened last year after our star loan man Lee Hendrie was accused of getting one of their players sent-off. Fittingly, my task to Rob was to get the word 'Hendrie' into his chat with Neil Warnock. He obliged.

So, a good three points and we have turned into media men! Well, nearly.

"Me and Alexis kitted out in Stoke gear…it was cold!"

9 February 2008. Wolverhampton Wanderers (away)

Having stopped in Stratford on the Friday, I met Dad and Aunty Isabelle at Molinuex. The ground is a tremendous sight. Decked out in the club colours of gold it stands out like a sore thumb. Somehow, I arrived at the exact same time as Dad. As I walked out of my car in our usual parking space, I nearly got run over by the crazy man! (only kidding Dad)

Stoke had sold their full allocation of tickets for this big match. After the 0-0 draw earlier in the season, there was far more optimism this time that we could win the derby. I live just down the road from Stafford and on the whole a Stafford lad is either Stoke or Wolves (or if they are unlucky Stafford Rangers). For many people, this is the biggest match of the campaign. Wolves hate us. We hate Wolves. So much, that we lovingly call them Wanky Wanderers!

With Fuller late arriving from Jamaica, Pulis stuck him on the bench and gave Gallagher his first appearance since returning from Blackburn. Gallagher's partner Sidibe benefited from a woeful back pass, rounded the keeper and crossed the ball right on the head of Delap. We were 1-0 up after four minutes! Following Delap's molehill incident at home to the Wolves, it was made even sweeter!

Wolves were guilty of some horrendous misses but turned the game around either side of half time. A sloppy equaliser in first half injury time was followed by Salif Diao falling asleep in the 47th minute, allowing Andy Keogh to make it 2-1. Awful Stoke. How can you throw it away like this?

Seconds later though, an incisive breakaway saw Whelan (making his first start) feed Lawrence who cracked in a right footer from the edge of the area. What a thriller! Back level.

The turning point came on the hour mark. Fuller entered the field of play at the expense of Gallagher who had put in a decent shift. Sidibe and Fuller are a beautiful partnership. Mama flicks on the ball and Ric runs with it. Pretty simple but it works.

A Lawrence corner was met by the head of Sidibe. It was surely a goal. No! What a save! Who was there though? Leon Cort. Three years ago, Leon's brother Carl scored a highly controversial equaliser at the same end of the ground against Stoke in the 94th minute to dent our play-off aspirations. How fitting that Leon has gone and scored himself. Despite my jubilation, I couldn't help but feel for Sidibe. The poor bloke goes and puts a goal on a plate for Delap, and then sees a goal bound header stopped by a world-class save. Is he destined never to score?!

The goal meant quarter of an hour of nail-biting. We were surely home and dry until Keogh waltzed passed Diao and the former Liverpool man stuck out a leg. Before Keogh even hit the ground, every Stoke supporter looked at the referee anticipating him to blow for a penalty. Amazingly, he didn't. The ball fell to Fuller 30 yards from his own goal and we could celebrate. The points were safe.

As he continued running with the ball towards, what we thought was the corner flag, we suddenly realised we might score a fourth. Bang. Goal! It was an astonishing individual goal, which sealed the most precious of victories. I think I even saw some Wolves fans applauding (a true rarity). What a way to empty the ground. Virtually the last kick of the game meant all the remaining Wolves fans quickly scampered out of the ground in disgust.

Beaming smiles were seen throughout the concourse. This was our first win at Molineux for twelve seasons. We were going to be singing until the early hours- make no mistake about it.

Those smiles were quickly wiped off our faces and replaced by horror when we came out of the stand. The Wolves fans who had left early (and who we hoped were eating their hot-dogs by now) were waiting for us and were aiming rocks at us. I thought these days had left English football?

It was very sad to see, especially when you have young children and elderly women walking about. What have they (or anyone else for that matter) done to deserve this? Absolutely nothing.

The three of us bit the bullet and made a dash for it towards our car, shielding our heads as we ran. Naively, I was still wearing my Stoke shirt and was politely told by a Wolves fan to take it off. Good plan! As we got to our cars, a running army of Wolves fans passed us towards the train station.

God knows what happened there. I just wanted to get away. All I wanted was to go to a football match!

February 12 2008. Southampton (home)

Alexis had made her way up to a cold Staffordshire for this. It was her first experience of a night match and what a game to choose! Stoke's Chief Executive, Tony Scholes, had made a superb offer to non-season ticket holders as a thank-you for their support. A buy one-get-one-free deal, whereby anyone who bought a ticket for tonight's match gets a ticket for Friday's game against Scunthorpe free of charge!

The result of this was a healthy attendance of nineteen and a half thousand supporters- our largest home crowd for a league match this season. After Fuller's superb display from the bench at Wolves, he returned to the starting line-up.

However, it was our pin-up (and Alexis' favourite player) Liam Lawrence who stole the show. Three of his perfectly directed corners resulted in goals. Firstly, Southampton defender Darren Powell contrived to screw his clearance into the back of his own net, before Shawcross rose highest to meet the ball and put us 2-0 up after 35 minutes.

Two goals to the good approaching half-time. This is easy! As Lawrence trotted over to take another corner we hoped for another. What we got was a miracle! Every millimetre of the 6 foot 4" Malian Mama Sidibe was needed as he bulleted the ball past the 'keeper to send the crowd and his team-mates into ecstasy! After six months of waiting, he is finally on the score sheet. He believed it would happen and here is the day.

At last! It has only taken him 1914 minutes (otherwise translated as 24 starts and a substitute appearance) to get his goal. It's a good job he's good at everything else. Amazingly, despite that statistic, I think Sidibe is fantastic. Stoke are a completely different team without him, and we often fail to adapt our play to accommodate life without him. Up until tonight's match, we have lost just one game all season with Mama in the team. Without him we have crumbled to five defeats. That tells you everything!

Half time, 3-0 up. This is brilliant! The half-time entertainment saw me firstly grab a hot cup of bovril to warm me up and then watch opposing supporters try and hit the cross bar from 20 yards out. A Southampton fan was asked what he made of the match so far to which his response was "We're gonna win 4-3!" Dream on mate.

OK, maybe I spoke a little too early. Within 10 seconds of the restart the strong Stern John rifled in a stupendous volley which looped over Simmo in the goal and into the back of the net from 30 yards. From nothing, Southampton had a lifeline. Nine minutes later, he was at it again. Having already gone close to another, John slipped the ball underneath Simmo to make Stoke's lead perilous.

Wave upon wave of attack from the Saints meant I was expecting the worst. Perhaps that fan was right. They are going to win 4-3. Slumped in my chair I couldn't believe what I was seeing. I normally sit pensively on the edge of my seat awaiting the next attack. I just couldn't anticipate us doing anything here- we had surely let it slip.

As the minutes ticked by without any further goals I began to realise we might actually hold onto all the points. Having nearly thrown it away, all may not be lost.
Although a three goal lead would be nice, the points are the main thing.

After four minutes of injury time, almost in slow motion, the referee glanced at both his watches and blew his whistle for the final time. The journey is over at last! That was a long 90 minutes of action but well worth it. Mama's headed goal had secured it all.

A win on Friday and we are top of the league!!

"A smiling Mama Sidibe with my Dad"

15 February 2008. Scunthorpe United (away).

At 7.00 on Wednesday morning, having recovered from the Southampton match, Alexis and I made our way up to Scotland. A business trip is always good fun, it changes the routine, and it is much more enjoyable when you are with the one you love.

Having been in the car for the best part of five hours, we eventually arrived in Edinburgh, saw a couple of customers, went to a couple of pubs and then went to see the big match. Hibernian v Gretna! I am awful. If there is a football match on I will watch it. I have seen football matches in England, Cyprus, Scotland, Wales, Iceland, Australia, Malta, France, Austria, Italy and no doubt other countries! It is all about seeing the language of football across the globe- I love it!

Anyway, having witnessed Hibs win 4-2, we drove across to Glasgow for a day (visiting Parkhead and Ibrox in the process) before coming down the M6 on the afternoon of the Scunthorpe match.

We were pretty warn out after a busy few days, but nothing was going to stop me from possibly seeing my boys go top of the pile!

Scunthorpe arrived bottom of the table and this was seen as a must win game if we are to really challenge for promotion. Due to FA Cup ties and strange decisions, this match was only announced two weeks ago, which prompted the club to implement the BOGOF offer. Following Tuesday's win, we broke the 20,000 barrier.

Settling down in our seats, we were quickly standing up ranting and raving. Dozy defending from Cort allowed former striker Paterson to nip in and score his first professional goal at the Britannia Stadium (in his tenth game at the ground).

It was a cruel blow and it was to get worse. Sidibe, the goalscoring hero from Tuesday, allowed centre back Jack Hobbs to run unchallenged and head home a simple second for Scunny. A disastrous start. We hadn't even begun to play.

The rest of the half wasn't any better and with us attacking the away end in the second half, there wasn't much hope. We tend to attack the Boothen End in the second half, as the supporters' enthusiasm contributes to sucking in goals at crucial times (at least that's what Brian Clough would say).

The players were sent out early for the remaining 45 minutes- and were greeted to a huge roar from the home support. Simmo arrived in goal to huge applause and despite the awful first half showing, there was still belief amongst the fans that we could turn this one round.

It took eight minutes before we had our first chance. The ball fell to Lawrence who fired across the keeper to bring us back into the match. While the celebrations went on, Pulis surreptitiously dragged off the poor Diao and brought Cresswell on.

Within a couple of minutes, we were back up celebrating although Fuller's header was ruled out due to a marginal offside.

The crowd were really beginning to believe that this was the time when we were to reach the summit. Soon after, substitute Cresswell justified the decision to bring him on by firing in an equaliser. Trademark skills from Fuller on the right touchline saw him pull the ball back to Cressy who fired the ball home. From 2-0 down, there now only seemed one winner…us!!

Five minutes later we had done it. Again, it was Fuller's skills that created it. Dancing past four players he used his head and put the ball on a plate for Lawrence who merely had to touch the ball to grab his second of the night. The ultimate comeback was complete.

The chants of "We are top of the League" immediately rang round the stadium and we also had a few renditions of the classic "City on top of the League", sung to the tune of a famous Status Quo track.

Smiles were back on faces, and we are getting closer to where we belong. The top flight!

We saw the victory out, and finished the week with incredible stats of ten goals scored and six conceded! The main stat though was nine points. How vital could these be?

23 February 2008. Ipswich Town (home)

Having only opened the 'away stand' to some supporters twice in the ten year history of the Britannia Stadium, the Ipswich fixture saw Stokies in there for the second game running. It makes such a difference for our players to run out to their own supporters both sides of the tunnel. You see, our ground is unique. Rather than having a traditional tunnel on the half way line, ours was stuck in the corner. It means that our 'keeper has a very long jog to reach the Boothen End every match!!

A bumper crowd of 23,563 (swelled by 5,000 free tickets from Britannia) came to the ground to witness the table toppers in action. Having won four games on the spin, our luck was surely going to change at some point. The main talking point was the signing of keeper Marton Fulop on loan from Sunderland. Finally, Simmo's place as our number one seemed to be under serious pressure.

Prior to the match a bust was unveiled of our all time record goalscorer, John Ritchie. Ritchie sadly passed away a year ago but will never be forgotten by those who saw him play or have merely heard of his exploits. A great hero being remembered in the right way.

Pulis decided that Fulop hadn't had enough training time so stuck him on the bench. Seeing him warm-up you could tell immediately that he is a keeper. He is bloody huge!!

Ipswich are not a team to be taken lightly. Having gone the entire season without an away win, they have won their last two away from Portman Road and have catapulted themselves into the play-off zone.

Their big bulky striker Alan Lee had a glorious chance in the first half. Having controlled well, he turned ten yards from goal and with the goal gaping he somehow blazed over. It was a real let off, and Stoke were to make Ipswich pay in the best way possible.

The windy conditions were making life difficult and Fuller forced a defender into playing the ball into Lawrence's path 35 yards from goal. With no teammate to pass to, he let fly with an almighty strike which flew into the top corner. It was a goal worthy of winning any match, and one which kept us top of the table.

Ipswich manager Jim Magilton, like Dave Jones earlier in the season, was getting frustrated at the multi-ball system, and decided to get rather irate at the referee. This resulted in the Irishman being sent to the stand- a decision which rather took the puff out of Ipswich.

We held on with relative ease to maintain our position looking down on the remaining 23 teams. What a wonderful feeling!

26 February 2008. Preston North End (away)

Having won five games on the bounce, optimism was high at the club. A healthy following of 2,000 Stokies made the trip to Lancashire. Dad and I decided to combine it with a business trip. I work for a trophy company, and often go out 'on the road' selling items. It seemed perfectly logical to get my petrol paid, see some customers and get the big match in at the same time (with the blessing of the big cheese, of course).

After visits to Southport, Leyland and Preston centre, we arrived at the ground in great time. Preston's Deepdale is home to the National Football Museum. It has almost become a ritual to visit the museum on our annual visits to the stadium and this occasion was no different. An hour of looking at old memorabilia was fantastic and Dad's old memories brought the old days to life for me. How times have changed!

After little food all day I dabbled in a balti pie and Bovril. It kept me nice and warm! We assumed that Fulop would be starting the game after Simmo had a few dodgy moments against Ipswich. Having met Simmo's best mate in Southport earlier in the day though, it transpired that Fulop had been recalled by Sunderland and we had now signed Carlo Nash from Wigan instead! What a fiasco. What must Simmo be thinking? We get a Hungarian international in who has probably been at the club for a shorter period of time than anyone in our history, and we subsequently sign another keeper instead!

We waited with baited breath then for the line up. The bloke on the tannoy (who deserves to be named and shamed as Adam Catterall) ran through the Stoke team at 100mph, leaving us with no chance of catching the line up and just hearing him laugh at his superb winding up. Good one mate!

It turned out that Nash hadn't actually signed in time, so Simmo was in goal (again) and we didn't have a keeper on the bench because Russell Hoult had joined Notts County on loan (are you keeping track of this?!)

A promising start to the match was halted when Shawcross gave away a silly free-kick on the half way line. A long hopeful punt wasn't dealt with and Richard Chaplow (who nearly broke Andy Wilkinson's leg a couple of years ago) tapped in for his first goal in the best part of two years.

It was a shocking goal to concede, and what an awful player to score it. The bald headed midfielder was at it again within a few minutes. Another free-kick conceded by Shawcross was knocked to Chaplow, who struck the ball low past Simmo for 2-0 before half-time.

What a kick to the kidneys this was. After our great winning streak, I suppose we felt invincible. It certainly wasn't the case! Fuller was being chopped down left, right and centre yet the 22 year old referee (yes, 22) bottled any decision to send off a player for it. It was weak refereeing throughout.

Somehow Fuller missed three one-on-one chances but our best chance fell to the in form Lawrence. Delap danced into the penalty area in the opening minutes of the second half. Just as he was losing his footing he passed to Lawrence who had an open goal but dallied too long and shot straight at a defender. What an incredible miss!

Centre back Leon Cort was trying to help us onto the score sheet but one attack saw him crumple in agony. All Stokies looked worried as three physios treated him on the pitch. Despite this, the referee seemed more concerned about where the bounce-ball would be taken from.

It was complete ignorance from him and summed up a bad night. All that was left was to trudge out of the ground still in the knowledge that we remained top of the league (because the other teams weren't playing) but we had blown a great chance.

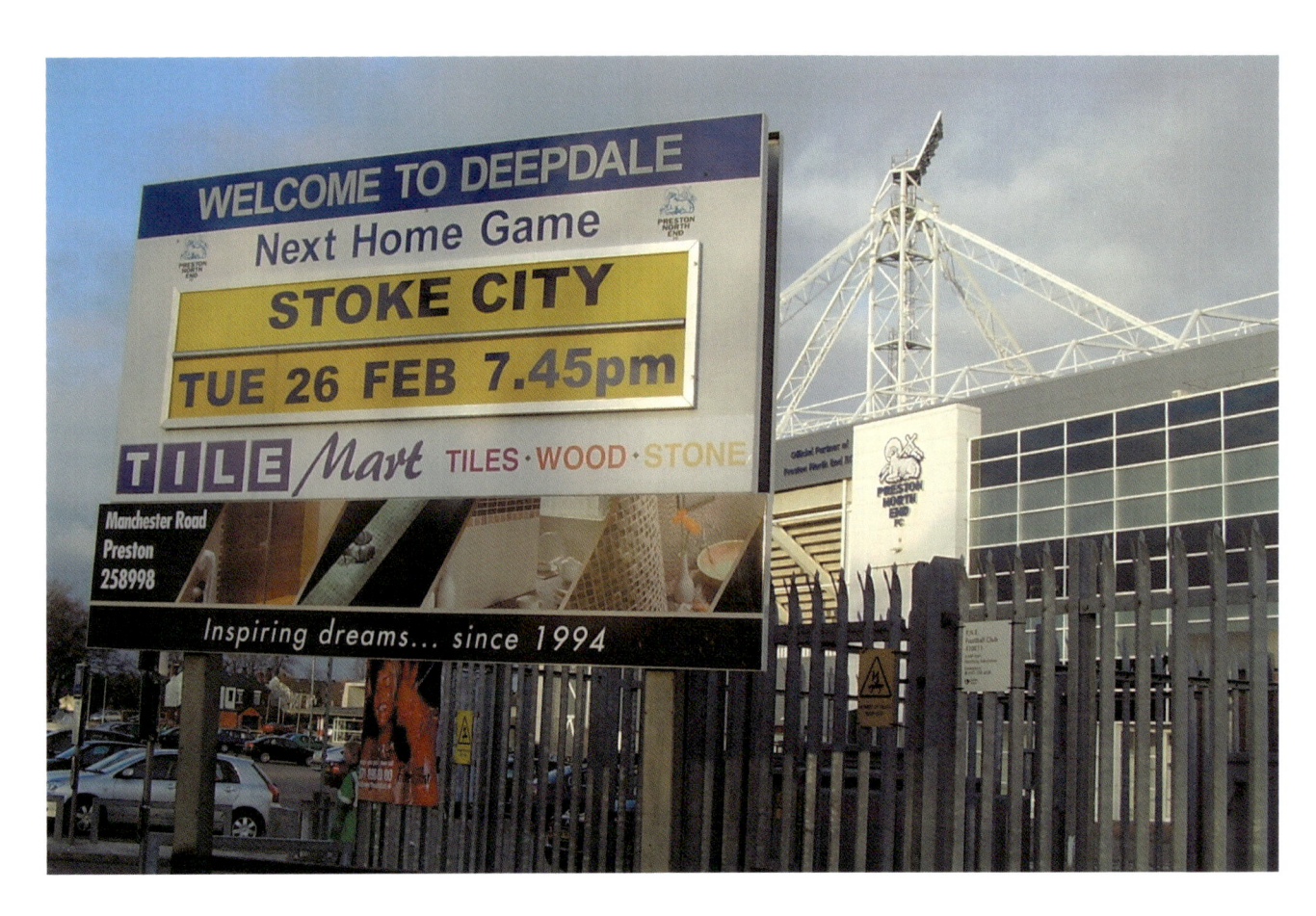

"At least we made it to the right match"

2 March 2008. Queens Park Rangers (away)

Despite our defeat in our final game of February, Tony Pulis was awarded the Championship Manager of the month award. This comes with a mixed blessing. It is widely accepted in the Football League, that there is a curse that comes with the award. Generally, a manager receives it and then the team loses the next game. To make matters even more interesting, Liam Lawrence had been named as officially the best player in the league for February (an award I fully agree with).

This match brought back horrible memories from last season. We went into the final game of the season needing a win by a better goal difference than Southampton to make the play-offs. The match was at Loftus Road, but in the sunshine, we messed it up and only managed a draw. With the games quickly running out, this was just as important.

The SKY cameras had moved the match to a Sunday, and to make matters worse, it was Mothering Sunday. Sorry Mum, I will see you later! Dad picked me up from Alexis' house, and we made it down to London for the quarter past one kick off.

My cousin Tim, who lives in Barnet, had a ticket for the match and was accompanied by his Mum (Aunty Isabelle). It's always nice to see Tim, although he could have chosen a better day for his upcoming wedding- Play Off Final day! We just have to make sure we go up automatically!!

The palaver regarding our goalkeeper situation continued. It was announced prior to the match that Nash wouldn't be signing until next week due to an injury to Wigan's number one, so we recalled Hoult from his loan spell and stuck him on the bench.

We nearly had the perfect start. A Lawrence corner was met by the head of Sidibe but the ball somehow struck the underside of the bar and came back into play. As we were all wondering how the ball didn't go in, QPR came racing forward on a counter attack. Without the suspended Delap in midfield, we allowed Mikele Leigertwood far too much space and he made us pay with a crisp strike into the bottom corner from 25 yards.

That's football for you- one second we could be 1-0 up yet we find ourselves a goal down.

For the first time, I was sitting at a match next to Andy and Chris. We couldn't believe the ridiculous dropping off by our midfield and defence. It was a stupid goal to concede.

Things were to get worse before the end of the half. A deep cross saw two defenders drift towards the ball. The knock down from Vine allowed the completely unmarked Leigertwood to smash home his second from six yards. Again, poor defending had let us down.

The pressure was getting to everyone. We were making silly mistakes and Griffin strangely went for the ball in a two-footed fashion. The QPR player was a good couple of yards away so it seemed odd that Griffin decided to do this. No harm done though. Or so we thought! Referee Andy d'Urso raced over as though Griff had broken the lad's leg (which he clearly hadn't) and issued a straight red card. It was one of those moments where you actually stand there with your mouth open in shock at the decision. There was no way in a month of Sunday's (quite an apt saying bearing in mind the day) that it was a foul, yet alone a bloody sending off!

All of this was still in the first half, and most Stokies were so busy shouting abuse at the referee that Fuller's effort that struck the post went unnoticed.

There was very little chance that we would turn this one round. Lawrence was having a stinker but he had a chance to prove why he had been named as player of the month with a well positioned free-kick. His feeble effort struck the base of the wall, QPR broke and made it 3-0. It was all over.

Despite decent substitute performances from Gallagher and Lewis Buxton (whose three appearances this season have all come in front of the SKY cameras) the match was all over for us. Fuller was doing his best to grab a goal, and the Stokies were in good voice.

It was all to no avail. We have seen this before with Stoke. I don't want to see it again. We are slowly throwing away a wonderful opportunity of promotion. Perhaps this will be our blip over. I certainly hope so.

8 March 2008. Burnley (home)

After the pair of damaging defeats, it was imperative we picked up three points against a decent Burnley side. A healthy away following made the trip down from Lancashire, and they were confident that their side (on the fringe of the play-offs) could cause an upset against us.

In horrible conditions, we finally saw the debut of Carlo Nash who had completed his long protracted move from Wigan, and immediately ousted Simmo in between the sticks. Another new face was that of Chris Riggott who had joined on loan from Middlesborough and partnered Leon Cort in the centre of defence in place of Shawcross.

Nash's first task was to pick the ball out of his net. Former Stokie James O'Connor found himself with the ball just outside the area. This in itself was a rarity, he normally finds himself in a very defensive midfield position. As three players converged round him, Kyle Lafferty had been left free by Griffin (who had his red-card suspension from QPR overturned). O'Connor spotted the unmarked left winger, fed him and he duly scored to send the away fans dancing round like lunatics.

Two defeats, and now losing this one. Promotion is looking a long way away at the moment. We need to buck our ideas up. Sadly, we weren't bucking up those ideas. A bland performance continued well into the second half. Burnley sub Andy Cole (previously a treble winner with Manchester United) was superbly denied by Nash late on, and that save gave us all a glimmer of hope that we could nick something from the game.

A hopeful long ball skipped along on the wet surface. It was a straight race between the slow Cresswell and Jon Harley. Cresswell managed to get it but was bundled down by the defender. With no hesitation, the referee pointed to the spot. We had been handed a lifeline.

Lawrence wiped the rain from his eyes, picked up the ball, and placed it on the spot. As he stepped up to take the shot, he ran over the ball because (as he admitted after the match) he didn't want to receive another yellow card from the referee for taking the penalty before the whistle was blown. How level headed of him in such a pressure situation!

With the referee's whistle firmly blown, Lawrence stepped up with purpose. The goalkeeper dived the right way but was beaten. The ball struck the post but hit the keeper on the back of his head and rolled into the net. A bizarre penalty but a goal. That is the main thing!

After 90 minutes of no attacking intent, we spent the three minutes of stoppage time bombarding the Burnley goal and we were unlucky not to see one of our strikes go in. It would have been rough justice on Burnley though who looked a decent side.

I can't say I'm particularly over the moon after that point, but at least we picked something up from the match. We have two massive away games this week, neither of which I particularly fancy us to get much out of. However, last time we played Burnley, we drew a dull match and went on a twelve match unbeaten run in the league.

A similar run should see us gain promotion!

11 March 2008. Norwich City (away)

A potentially season defining two match stint started on the other side of the country in East Anglia. This was going to turn out to be one of the longest days of my life. I decided (just as I did at Preston) that I would go on one of my agreed business trips, and save some petrol money.

Dad and I set off just before 8.00 in the morning, twelve hours ahead of kick-off! It took us the best part of three and a half hours to even reach Peterborough, before visiting King's Lynn and then onto Norwich, which we reached at 5.30PM.

As top cook Delia Smith is a majority shareholder at Norwich, we resisted the temptation to have a pre-match curry, and opted to try one of her 'big match specials'. Today, it was a superb meat and mushy pea pie. I couldn't have asked for anything better. It certainly warmed us up after walking in the driving rain for 20 minutes from the car to the ground.

Despite being second in the league, we had sold a paltry 351 tickets for this match, so we were going to have to be in fine voice to make ourselves heared over the 23,000 home supporters.

Ironically, for the second away game running, we found ourselves sitting next to Andy and Chris, and we met up with Rob who had come over on the coach. Apparently the heating controls had broken on the coach, so everyone had come off with rosy cheeks and sweat pouring down their brow- I think they were glad to get out in the open air. I wasn't, it was absolutely freezing.

Norwich had lost their last game and by all accounts were absolutely woeful. Their manager Glenn Roeder (who is far from the most charismatic Manager around) had torn into his team and was expecting more for the visit of Stoke. He got more, Norwich came out of the blocks flying. Nash had to be in top form and made some good saves, although his kicking was looking a bit suspect in the swirling wind.

This game summed up the Championship. With the respective league positions, it is a game we should win, but it doesn't work like that. There are no easy games, and Norwich were giving us great problems. Fuller had been left on the bench after a run of indifferent form. It was a big call by the gaffer, but after a hectic start, the front two of Sidibe and Cresswell were beginning to get more involved, and we finished the first half the stronger of the two teams.

The turning point was when Fuller came on for the awful Diao. Diao just is not match fit at the moment- why can't the manager see it?! The introduction of Fuller gave the players and supporters a belief that we could do this job, and get three points.

Within five minutes we had got a goal. A trademark long throw from Delap was flicked on by Sidibe, and his header looped over the advancing keeper and into the back of the net. Cue a great mental amongst the clutch of Stokies, as the players ran over to celebrate with us. After our indifferent run, perhaps things were at last changing for the better?

We had to endure strong Norwich pressure, and it was surely going to tell as the ball fell to our nemesis Jamie Cureton three yards from goal. Cureton has a horrible habit of always scoring against us. This time he somehow completely missed the target and Norwich's big chance had gone. We had won!!

We eventually got home having driven for nine and a half hours! It was well worth it, and after our two promotion rivals Watford and Bristol City drew against each other, the night was made even better.

Roll on Saturday…

15 March 2008. Watford (away)

With Stoke second in the table, and Watford just one place behind, there was no doubting the importance of this match. As soon as Dad picked me up from Alexis' house, the adrenaline started running. I was looking forward to the match, but also extremely nervous. I had the feeling it would be a very long 90 minutes.

Our hopes of success were hardly helped by the announcement of Rob Styles as the main man in charge. Now Styles is hardly greeted with the most excitement by any football fan in the country, least of all Stoke. Back in 2000, we were playing a vital play-off semi final match against Gillingham in Division Two. Having gone into the second leg 3-2 up, Styles decided to send off two of our players leaving us no chance of holding on. We eventually lost on the evening 3-0. That prat will never be forgiven.

He came out of the tunnel half an hour prior to kick off for his routine warm-up. He immediately trotted over to the Stoke fans and shrugged his shoulders as we booed and shouted obscenities at him. Watford fans applauded him around the ground in the hope that their nice welcome might contribute him to assist them through the match.

No such chance. This was the first opportunity for us Stoke supporters to say goodbye to former captain John Eustace who joined Watford on January transfer deadline day. He has been doing so well at Vicarage Road that he has now been appointed their captain. He was pulling the strings for them, he was back to his best. We were being murdered by Watford yet kept them at bay until the turning point.

Eustace went in for a challenge on Cresswell and caught his knee. Styles (wanting to be the centre of attention as ever) raced over and immediately issued a straight red card. This was inside the first 25 minutes too! Brilliant, we have a majority of the game against ten men. We sang a (cruel) song for Eustace as he trudged off the playing field, "Super Johnny Eustace". The poor bloke must have felt like crying.

We didn't really exert our one man advantage, and it was Watford looking the more likely. Pulis had decided to change formation for the first time this season, with five playing at the back. This meant that our new signing Jay Bothroyd from Wolves made his debut in a free role, roaming just behind Fuller. Bothroyd scored against our reserves just the other week, but was clearly lacking match fitness for such a high tempo match as this one. At least we were keeping a clean sheet.

I have a horrible habit of chewing gum during matches to calm down my tension. Having chewed more than normal I decided to throw my gum away. I checked I wasn't going to hit anyone, but my glasses must have been playing tricks on me as I smacked a steward plush on the top of his head. I quickly hid my face!

In the second half, Griffin went in for a challenge and won the ball. As the ball rolled away, it just brushed his little finger. Our friend Mr Styles thought it would be a cracking idea to award a penalty for it. All sides of the ground were bemused at the award for what Styles described to Griffin as: "It just hit your hand".

Nevertheless, a penalty had been given and we had to deal with it. In such an important fixture, I didn't envy the pressure on Henderson's shoulders as he stepped up to the mark. I kept reminding myself how he had missed a penalty at Bristol City on Tuesday.

He fired it to Nash's right, the keeper guessed right and the penalty was saved. The rebound was cleared and we could all breath a sigh of relief and jump around like monkeys!

We had just one powder puff effort on target all match, but with West Brom (who are now referred to as West Brazil as their supporters believe they are the best team in the world) and Bristol City losing at home, we crept our way onto top of the table again.

Nowhere near the prettiest match I ever seen, but extremely tense. We held on for a point that I would have snapped someone's hand off before kick off.

Things are going to go down to the wire. We are top on goal difference and three points ahead of third placed Watford (but they have a game in hand).

These next seven games are the biggest games in our history

22 March 2008. Blackpool (home)

With it being the Easter period, I had the luxury of a day off on Friday- spent doing absolutely nothing with Alexis. I love lazy days!

I knew there was a problem as soon as I got onto the motorway. All the overhead matrixes were reporting long delays on the M6, and the radio was saying that it was shut southbound.

The obvious problem with this was that all Blackpool players and supporters would be coming that way. Would we have a game at all?

Dad, Aunty Isabelle and I pulled into the car park at the stadium in good time. As we always do, we listened to Radio Stoke for the line-up as read out by first team coach Dave Kemp. With three top players suspended, this was going to be tough. No Fuller, no Lawrence and no Shawcross. Ouch!

After the line-up had been announced, John Acres, the presenter reported a delay of half an hour to the kick off due to the accident on the M6. This meant a lot of kicking of heels!

Luckily, I picked up a copy of our fanzine *The Oatcake* and wandered over to the Stanley Matthews statue which overlooks the wasted land which used to house our previous stadium, The Victoria Ground. As I flicked through the pages, I was treated to reading Rob's tales of his favourite ten games. A perfect setting to do so. It is such a shame that I never saw Stan play.

Having kicked enough heels, I decided to make my way into my fading red seat in Block 20 of the Boothen End. I have never seen the ground so full half an hour prior to kick off!

The delay to the match was only because of the referee being stuck in the queue on the motorway. Supporters and players made it on time. The setback to kick off will now result in a fine for Stoke, and it is the first time it has happened since the final game of last century against Oldham.

A promising Stoke start saw Salif Diao hobble off and we lost our rhythm. Now, Blackpool gave us a run for our money back in December and I certainly wasn't expecting this one to be an easy ride.

Indeed, at seven minutes past four (in the 37th minute), they took the lead. Ben Burgess's shot was being comfortably stopped by Nash in between the sticks. However, Cort put his lanky leg in the way and the ball spun into the back of the net.

With us being top of the league, we cannot afford to drop points in this one. Ben Burgess is my favourite non-Stoke player. Back in 2002, in the crucial Division Two play-off final, he scored an own goal for his team Brentford to help us on our way to victory. I have cheered his name ever since that day. How dare he then have the cheek to actually score for his own team against us?

It really was a lacklustre performance in the first half and we deserved to be behind. We are going through a sticky patch at completely the wrong part of the season. Luckily, Hull aside, all the other teams around us are going through a similar patch and the half time scorelines reflect this.

The boys came out of the tunnel early (clearly after an ear bashing from Pulis) to a tremendous roar from the crowd. "Come on Stoke" was the cry.

An early goal would set us up nicely. A corner was swung in by Gallagher to the far post. Inexplicably, my mate Burgess decided to head it back into the danger area and Cort stabbed the ball home. Two minutes gone, we effectively have a whole half of football to get one more goal.

Surprisingly, it was Blackpool who came closest to a winner. We never really got going again. It was a disappointing goal, but at least we had salvaged a point and the other results meant we stayed top of the league.

Some of the fans booed the team off. What a disgrace. Dad and I confronted the bloke behind us, whose response was "We're only top because Bristol City lost". Yes, quite right, so Bristol have lost all their games throughout the season have they? Numpty!

Six games to go. We need to stick together.

"Me and Rob at Sir Stan's statue"

29 March 2008. Sheffield Wednesday (away)

Alexis, Gilley and Alana had popped off to Mallorca with their family for a week. Work constraints meant I was unable to attend apart from the weekend. Much to the disgust of everyone, I decided to stay in the wet surroundings of England to go to this match. All my taunting to Gilley would have to be done via text!

This was the first time back at Hillsborough for super Glenn Whelan. Just to remind you Gilley, he is now running OUR midfield! We were also buoyed by debuts for the Premiership pair of Stephen Pearson (Derby) and Shola Ameobi (Newcastle) who had arrived on loan.

We had finally reached the stage in the season when there were categorically no more signings allowed. We had to make do with the bunch we had. They have done superbly so far, we are top of the league!

Having travelled up on the coach, Rob, Steve and I were optimistic we could turn around our indifferent run of form. In the driving rain we nipped into a Chippy for a bite to eat. Not the best idea- we ended up standing outside the ground for five minutes while I finished my tray of chips off.

Soaking wet, we took our place and the match started off with Sheffield Wednesday looking the most likely. Somehow they hit the bar when it was easier to score and Ameobi and Dickinson went into the book.

Pearson was looking lively on the left wing, and the man who he had replaced on the flank capitalised on a tremendous cross to send 3,000 Stokies wild. Richard Cresswell had reverted to his preferred forward position, and he cleverly flicked home past the 'keeper.

The computerised screen to our right kept giving us score updates around the Championship. Much to everyone's amazement, bottom club Colchester were winning 2-0 at our rivals West Brom Could this be the day when we pull clear?

Cresswell missed a superb chance early in the second half when he completely mis-timed a header in front of the travelling fans. Will we regret that opportunity?

The answer came in the 82nd minute. Loanee Franck Songo'o fired home after a mistake from the terrible Griffin to equalise for Wednesday. It was utter heartbreak. Pulis had played his substitute cards already- we had no attacking threat remaining.

Infact, it was the home side who were looking the more likely- surely we can't lose this one?!

We ended up settling for the point, which was no use at all. The doom and gloom suddenly became shock on our return journey home. All is explained here by my article in The Sentinel:

I refer you all to this particular rule from 'The Regulations of the Football League Limited' handbook:

47.3.1 A maximum of 5 loan Players (either Short Term or Long Term) can be named in the sixteen players listed on a team sheet for any individual Match.

Surely, in a week whereby loan signings were at the forefront of everybody's mind, Sheffield Wednesday would have the ingenuity to check the rules regarding their availability.

Clearly they didn't. By naming Kavanagh, Sahar, Bolder, Slusarski, Showumni and Songo'o in their sixteen, they made a mockery of regulation 47.3.1.

It is seeming increasingly likely that the league will follow the precedent they set in 2006 by just fining Sheffield Wednesday- the same way they dealt with Leeds United under similar circumstances.

The difference here though is that Leeds lost that particular game against Burnley, whereas Stoke dropped two vital points- ironically conceding a goal to one of these loanees.

There is absolutely no justice in this impending verdict in my eyes. Brian Laws manipulated the rules to suit him. He had options on the bench that shouldn't have been available to him (one of them, Showmuni, turned the game).

Stoke meanwhile had used their initiative and checked the regulations (which are easily available online to anyone in the world). In fact, they were without the quality options of Gallagher and Zakuani on the bench to coincide with the regulations.

Tony Scholes must argue our case as far as he can, as I believe we have a good shout for regaining the two points back. However, we know this won't happen, as the Football League are spineless and wouldn't dream of making such a landmark decision so close to the end of the campaign. It is a real shame.

Do Sheffield Wednesday deserve that extra point? No. How would Southampton feel if they went down by one point? This argument is far from over.

As for our new loanees. Pearson injected some much needed natural wing play on the left hand side. He could be a real gem in the coming weeks. We all know that Ameobi is a quality signing. In my eyes he is Mama who can score goals (although he didn't look too threatening on Saturday). With a week of training together, I am confident that the lads can all pull together and get the necessary three points against Palace on Monday.

Keep in there Stoke. We must believe!

So there you have it, perhaps there is some hope of a reprieve. Our only hope was for the Football League to clamp down and give us some points back. For the meantime, we must concentrate on Crystal Palace…

April 2008. Crystal Palace (home)

One win in seven games just isn't promotion form. Thankfully the teams around us seem to be dropping points as if it is the new fashion. It is imperative we halt this alarming poor run and pick up the points tonight in front of the SKY cameras.

I had woken up at 5.00 in the morning to drive up to the Britannia Stadium from Stratford and queue up in the freezing cold to obtain my ticket for the final away game of the season at Colchester.

With it being a potentially pivotal game in our history, a small allocation and Colchester's final game at Layer Road meant demand was high. Thus, Stoke had announced that tickets would only be on initial sale to supporters who have attended at least ten away games. Thankfully I was successful (I would have been gutted if my hard efforts went unrewarded) and I drove to work with a beaming smile on my face.

It seemed strange to return to the Brit almost twelve hours later for a much more important event. Much to the shock of everyone in the ground, Pulis decided to keep the returning Fuller on the bench and rushed Mama Sidibe back from a hamstring injury to partner Shola upfront.

It backfired horribly. We looked devoid of ideas in the final third of the pitch and clever wing play saw our poor full backs (Pugh and Griffin) lose out as Soares soared (excuse the obvious pun) to head home. If that wasn't bad enough, their centre back rifled home a peach of a volley into the back of the net on the stroke of halftime.

This was an almighty task now. My only hope was that we had turned around a similar deficit to Scunthorpe a couple of months ago. However, Palace are a much stronger side than Patto's struggling side.

We came back out intent on bringing ourselves back into the match. Everything we threw at Palace ended up in 'keeper Speroni's hands or went wide. The introduction of Bothroyd and Fuller livened things up but it just wasn't meant to be.

Irishman Whelan scored a contender for goal of the season with a volley from 25 yards which whistled into the back of the net but it wasn't enough.

I could barely bring myself to stand up at the final whistle. I was so deflated.

This is our best chance to get into the top flight of English football in my fifteen years of supporting the club. We are rapidly making a huge pig's ear of it. We need to turn things around quickly.

Don't let me down Stoke.

12 April 2008. Coventry City (away)

All week I had prepared for this one. After the agony of defeat against Palace, we needed to get three points to rekindle our automatic promotion hopes. With our recent form though I just couldn't see it.

However, with a backing of more than 3,000 Stokies, the lads should certainly have plenty of support. A couple of days before the match, it transpired that I wouldn't be amongst the 3,000. Alexis' parents had organised it so that the four of us (Alexis, her parents and myself) would be in an executive box. This was certainly different!

Arriving at the ground two hours prior to kick off, we settled down in the box alongside eight Coventry fans. I felt slightly outnumbered!

It was surreal, we had bar staff regularly popping in and checking we were OK for drinks. After our chicken and rice, I decided to pop outside and watch a bit of football (it was easy to forget that there was a match due to be played!)

I wish I had stayed inside. We were awful for the first half. The only bright point was that the two players who haven't been playing to the best of their ability in recent weeks (Griffin and Ameobi) were withdrawn due to injury.

Referee Uriah Rennie pointed to the spot on the half hour mark. Surrounded by Coventry fans, I knew what was coming. Duly, Elliot Ward sent Nash the wrong way and ran over to the Stoke fans to gloat. That made my half time pudding taste rather bitter.

I texted Rob and Dad (who were in the Stoke end) to gauge their thoughts on the half:
"*We are blowing it big time, shocking display*" and "*Very poor*", just about summed it all up.

I just couldn't see where a goal was coming from. Fuller had our first real shot and then picked the ball up on the half way line. Finally, we saw something we had been missing for the past couple of months. A trademark run from Ric saw him glide into the penalty area and, with three defenders around him, he drew a foul from one of them and won a penalty.

With his confidence high, he picked up the ball and placed it on the spot. Now, although I was in the Coventry end, it didn't bother me. All I cared about was this ball hitting the back of the net. Edging closer to the pitch, as Fuller walked up to the ball, I stood up and screamed out with a release of huge tension. It had gone in, to send the 3,000 Stokies crazy. It was a tremendous sight.

Being in a box is extremely bizarre. For the second half, there were just two of us braving the wintery conditions, with the others either drinking wine or peeking at the field of play through the comfort of double-glazing!

Stoke surprisingly brought on the magnificent Liam Lawrence midway through the second half. Normally the first name on the team sheet, he had defied the odds to be named in the sixteen despite a groin injury.
His class immediately shone. He was the one player who could carry the ball, pass it to feet, and take the pressure off the rest of the lads. Gary, whose box we were in for the day, turned to me and said he reminded him of Matt le Tissier. High praise indeed.

From the moment he entered the field, I knew we were heading for three points. We had turned around obvious defeat into a great chance of victory.

Cresswell picked up the ball and went on a raging run. His touch slightly eluded him and Coventry's keeper (Peter Schmeichel's son, Kasper) dived at his feet. The loose ball fell to Lawrence who calmly curled the ball home from the edge of the area.

I was lost in the moment. Standing up out of my chair and celebrating like a mad man! This could be the most crucial goal of the season. Lawrence was lost in the moment too. Ripping off his shirt like the Incredible Hulk, he whipped up the Stokies into a frenzy.

That was it. Coventry didn't look like threatening us for the remaining ten minutes. The points were ours, and with other results going our way, we had returned to the top of the table with just three games left. Wow, what a season this is unfolding into!

After the excitement of the activites on the field, I made my way to the Legends Bar (on my own, as nobody else really cared about the old Coventry players!). Alexis' Dad's mate Kirk Stephens used to be a popular player at Coventry and Luton Town. It was down to him that we were in the box for the day, and he looked after me, introducing me to ex-players in the bar.

I decided the most interesting people were Cyrille Regis, Micky Gynn, John Williams and Dave Bennett. I propped myself at the bar and had a beer with them. Cyrille turned to me and told me how sorry he was for me. The reason? Tony Pulis' style of football. Something he described as 'Neanderthal football". I don't think he was very impressed!! That said, he was a bit of a legend in his day so I wasn't going to disagree! At least we will have the money if we go up!

What a day. I have had the pleasure of meeting players who have won the FA Cup and also seen the boys do the business on the pitch.

The last port of call was the casino. The Ricoh Arena is like a little village. It has the pitch, an indoor live event arena, a top class restaurant, and the best part- the casino! It was incredible. Like something out of the movies.

We made our way down the escalator and grabbed a drink before Kirk whisked us into the Coventry City VIP area. He didn't want us to brush shoulders with the riff-raff!! In there, we were taught how to play roulette by Dave Bennett and were playing alongside the new owner of Nuneaton Borough. Add to this, the never ending supply of complimentary champagne and it was turning into a decent night. I could get used to this!

The whole gambling thing passed me by to be honest. I put the princely sum of twenty notes on to the table and gained a few quid in the process. It wasn't about gambling though. It was the experience.

And what an experience it was. Most importantly though….we are top of the league (again)!

"A healthy Stoke following"

19 April 2008. Bristol City (home)

Following on from the remarkable turnaround at Coventry, we had to follow it up with a victory in front of the SKY cameras against our near rivals Bristol City.

The euphoria surrounding the Coventry match had been somewhat tempered by midweek victories for West Brom and Hull which meant we had slipped from top to third in the table. However, with earlier results going our way, we knew going into this 5.20 kick off that a win would move us back into the automatic promotion spots. Do you understand?!!

A packed Britannia welcomed the teams onto the pitch after a bit of pre-match entertainment. Local station Radio Stoke had recently had a phone-in which an anonymous supporter named 'Pottermouth' had left a Battle Cry for the lads.

The Battle Cry, including lines such as "Do it for Josiah Wedgwood, and for a PMT bus" and "Do it for Dennis Smith and the old Victoria Ground" was played before kick off by the presenters of the show, and created an electric atmosphere.

I was feeling physically sick in the run up to this match. It was quite simply huge. Win and we are still in the hunt. Anything else and it could all be over and we would be putting up with the lottery of the play-offs.

Mama Sidibe returned to the starting line up, this eased my mind- he is, as I have mentioned before, simply crucial to our style.

This was Mama's day. The tension was slightly eased when Lawrence won a free kick out on the right. He swung it in himself, and Sidibe, facing away from goal, somehow managed to force the ball home off the back of his head.

It was a great start and everybody was delighted that Sidibe had got himself on the scoresheet. His previous two goals had resulted in 1-0 victories. We would take the same today!

Sidibe had different ideas though. Captain for the day, Rory Delap, broke up a Bristol attack and Fuller did enough to set Sidibe in the clear. Now, Mamady Sidibe breaking through one-on-one with the goalkeeper is not a sight that fills most Stokies with great confidence. Despite his excellent work rate, his finishing is pretty poor to say the least. When he calmly slotted the ball past the advancing Basso, the shock quickly turned into an almighty mental. Get in there!! We are going up!!

Belief was well and truly back amongst the Stokies during the half time period. As we watched the highlights of the goals in the concourse eating our pies, an almighty rendition of Delilah broke out. What will it be like if we gain promotion?

An offensive start to the second half saw Fuller get out the tricks and all was going along sweetly. That was until our friends from cider land won a corner and bloody Adebola scored against us. Again. As mentioned in the Coventry match, he always seems to score against us and we now had 25 minutes of nail biting!

The match swung from end to end, Shawcross cleared one off the line and the visiting fans were beginning to believe again. A draw would still move us up into the top two but it is the three points we really need.

Mum, who was only making her second Stoke appearance of the season could barely watch (this coming from someone who doesn't really have much care for football) but her singing of Stoke songs helped spur on the boys.

Goalscoring hero Sidibe was left crumpled with a serious looking ankle injury and was stretchered off to be replaced by loanee Ameobi late on. Pulis used all the tricks to try and run down the clock, bringing on Wilko- would this match ever end?

Finally, the referee looked at his watch for the final time and blew his whistle. It was the most incredible celebration at full time that I have ever seen. Coach Mark O'Connor raced onto the pitch and jumped into the arms of the delighted Dicko, who had a stormer.

I walked away firmly in the belief that we will now go up. What a turn around from two weeks ago.

As Pottermouth said, "Do it, do it Pulis, please do it".

Part one of the final three has been done.

26 April 2008. Colchester United (away)

What an occasion. Colchester's last ever game at their tiny Layer Road ground and possibly the moment Stoke step into the Premier League for the first time in their history.

It was Twenty-three years ago when we last played in the top flight of English football (seven months before I was born) and that heart-wrenching wait could finally be over. All we have to do is win and hope Hull slip up against Palace. If that happens, Tony Pulis' boys will be promoted!

Dad picked me up from Stratford and we made the three hour journey nice and early, getting to the ground three hours before kick off! This was a day that I was going to try and savour (despite the nerves).

I started by meeting the likes of Teddy Sheringham outside the ground and enjoying some banter with the Colchester fans while listening to the carnival like atmosphere surrounding Layer Road.

Having met Rob off his coach, we immediately stepped foot in the ground (an hour and a half prior to kick off). It was nice to get in the shade at last, the sun was baking!! Colchester, like Cardiff on the opening day, is open terraces, meaning supporters stand up, just like the good old days!

Stoke Chairman Peter Coates had kindly donated 500 Stoke scarves to be handed out to the fans, and it created a wonderful sea of red and white (including the stewards who had decided to wear the scarves, adding to the friendly atmosphere).

The players warmed up to a series of songs from the away fans. The tension was practically unbearable!

Having experienced the Layer Road toilets for the last time (thankfully, they are dire!) and eating a burger which resembled some kind of amalgamation of road killed pigeon and rat, I settled down in my position and watched the action unfold before me.

We started well, forcing numerous corners and their keeper into a couple of decent saves from Fuller. Then, disaster elsewhere. Hull had taken the lead at home to Palace. It was a real kick in the teeth. If they took all three points then we couldn't clinch promotion today.

That goal for Hull had subdued the fans somewhat, but news soon reached us that Palace had equalised. It was as though Stoke themselves had scored. With nothing much happening on the pitch at Layer Road, it was left to people informing us via radio, text, phone call or whatever means about the other game.

As our match drifted into stoppage time, a long Rory Delap throw was headed towards goal by Cresswell. His header was superbly saved by the keeper but Lawrence kept the ball alive. His cross-cum-shot was poked in by Cresswell from two yards to spark mayhem.

This was potentially the most important goal ever scored by Stoke in my lifetime. It made the half time interval very enjoyable. With no concourse in the away end, all the Stokies were singing songs on the terraces- "We are Going Up" might be slightly premature but if all the matches ended now, we would be doing so!!

The lads returned for the second half to one huge roar from the lucky 950 Stokies who had queued up to gain admission to this historic match.

The goal had given Stoke a tremendous boost. Fuller looked interested, and was doing his best to double the lead. One run culminated in him firing the ball across the goal, just missing Sidibe's lunging frame.

As the minutes flew by it was seeming increasingly likely that this was going to be the day. I was trying to curb my excitement but it was difficult. Promotion would mean everything. Speaking to John Acres on Radio Stoke the night before, he asked me how I would celebrate promotion. My answer? By crying!

I wasn't ashamed to admit it, but there was still a job to be done. The fourth official walked out with his little board to signal four additional minutes. Just four minutes!

With Lawrence and Ameobi playing for time near the corner flag, news filtered through of a goal in Hull. This was time to slump on the terraces. Hull had scored with just a few minutes remaining. It was agony but all we could affect was what was happening against Colchester.

At least we were winning. With just a couple of minutes left of the added on time, Colchester floated a ball into our area and Nash came flying out, flapping like an injured seagull. The ball nestled into the back of the net but before Colchester could celebrate, the referee disallowed it. Relief!!

As the ref blew the whistle, some of the players celebrated as though we had done it. In the stands we knew of Hull's scoreline so reacted rather mutedly. In all essence we have left ourselves just one point from promotion but it was an extremely strange sensation.

All that was left was to watch Colchester say goodbye to Layer Road. Dad and I were the final away supporters to leave the ground and decided it had been a good day. It could have been better had Palace held on for a draw but we did our bit.

Roll on the biggest match ever seen at the Britannia Stadium. Stoke City v Leicester City, for a place in the promised land!

"The sign tells you everything"

28 April 2008. Awards Evening.

Through my line of work, I found myself organising the trophies for the awards evening. Despite working to tight deadlines it was great fun, and I felt a real part of the night.

Ten of us descended upon the Britannia Stadium to celebrate the squad's achievements so far. With just one game left it was important not to get carried away but there was certainly cautious optimism from the Stoke players, not just to go up, but to also win the title.

We started off in the VIP lounge, enjoying a couple of drinks with the players before heading into the beautifully decked out Waddington Suite. Tony Waddington is considered our greatest ever manager, and helped us to our only triumph of note, the 1972 League Cup.

I was honoured to be given the task of presenting Nathaniel Wedderburn with a well-deserved Academy Player of the Year Award. The young, mountainous midfielder has a great future ahead of him.

Sitting on our table were Anthony Pulis and Jamaican international, Demar Phillips. Demar and I shared some banter, and decided to have a bet on the winner of goal of the season. I was adamant it would be Fuller's strike at Wolves while Demar plumped for Lawrence against QPR.

As the nominees were listed, both our goals were there, but Fuller's strike won, leaving me £10 better off. Not the most money I will ever win but satisfying nonetheless!

After Lawrence, Fuller and Shawcross shared the other awards, and the wonderful Mable won fan of the year, we were left to say goodbye to all the players, until we see them again on Sunday for the titanic battle!!

4 May 2008. Leicester City (home)

So, a season's hard efforts culminate in ninety minutes of football. After the Colchester roller coaster, it was simple. We had to obtain a point at home against relegation threatened Leicester to seal promotion. The only way we would miss out was a Hull victory and a defeat for ourselves.

Despite this seemingly easy task, the nerves were pumping for this one. I couldn't sleep on the Saturday night and come the morning of the match, I could barely talk, let alone eat!!

The pre match plans had been thrown into disarray when Middlesbrough decided to recall Chris Riggott at the last minute, which meant Andy Wilkinson would slot in at right back. Despite the loss of Riggott, Wilko is a hungry local lad, willing to give everything for the cause, and I was confident he wouldn't let us down.

The build up to the match was incredible. My cousin, Mike, had made the journey from New York just to watch this match. Aunty Isabelle and he were lucky enough to purchase two of the final tickets for the game, and Mum sat with me and Dad. It really was a family affair!!

The game itself was horrible. I couldn't enjoy one moment of it. Throughout the match, all I could think of was the possible prestige at the end of it. This had been labelled as Stoke's most important game in our history. It was hard to argue when we stand to gain a minimum of £60 million if we do gain promotion.

For goodness sake Stoke, don't mess it up!! Leicester defender N'Gotty was doing his best to subdue Fuller's threat, and Leicester's physical approach led to a serious looking injury to Wilko after 20 minutes. Striker Steve Howard went flying in and nearly ended up breaking his ankle, leading to the young man limping off. How the Leicester forward escaped a red card I will never know.

This enabled Lewis Buxton to come on for his fourth appearance of the season. In line with his other three matches, this one came in front of the SKY cameras. A quite incredible statistic!

It was not only ourselves who were playing for the points. Leicester were scrapping for their lives and needed a win to ensure their safety. A defeat (or even a draw) could lead to them slipping into the third flight of English football for the first ever time.

In the driving rain, things were beginning to get rather scrappy but it was Leicester who were looking the more likely to open the scoring. Just as a false rumour filtered through the stadium that Ipswich had scored against Hull, Leicester's captain McAuley struck the post with a header.

This was unbearable. I could hardly watch. The time was slowly ticking. As things stood, we were going up, but football is a funny old game. Things can change so quickly.

Then, in an instant, everything changed. Ipswich HAD scored. It was confirmed by the man in front of me who was listening to the radio and I had my own little merry dance. Surely now we were up?! At the same time, Leicester's rivals Southampton took the lead meaning the Foxes had to score to stay up!

What a final 20 minutes in store for us. Leicester manager Ian Holloway (despite having the same surname as Rob, absolutely no relation) chucked on extra ammunition, and they were playing with four upfront. What a test of nerve for our rearguard.

Thankfully we had Carlo Nash in goal. An incredible save from Hume led to a corner for Leicester. As it was swung in, Stearman's vicious header was acrobatically turned over. I was feeling sick. The thought of Hull losing had momentarily left my head.

It appeared that Leicester had given all they had. They had put in a good shift but it was looking like it wouldn't be enough. The outdated electronic scoreboard in the corner ticked over to the final five minutes and it dawned on the supporters how close we were. Many fans made their way to the bottom of the stand in preparation for an almighty pitch invasion. Please don't tempt fate!!

So, we entered the four minutes of added on time and news reached us that the final whistle had been blown at Ipswich. Hull had lost, meaning we were promoted!! Some idiots celebrated this by running onto the pitch, leading me to panic about points deductions (in such times, you always fear the worse!)

After the stewards had ushered the idiots off, it was real party time. The pitch was immediately flooded by delirious Stokies. I turned to Dad, hugged him and cried. Mum was there keeping back the tears (she doesn't even like football!!) The whole moment was a blur. I looked down at the pitch and noticed Mike and Aunty Isabelle down there. I legged it down the stairs and hugged them in joy. This was absolutely incredible.

About 15,000 Stokies had made their way onto the hallowed turf and the players (who had survived the onslaught of supporters) appeared at a balcony, waving at the gazing masses. Every one of these players had written themselves into folklore.

None more so than Dicko, who decided to scream at the top of his voice down the microphone and join in a rendition of Delilah. Classic stuff!

Despite not seeing a Stoke match for over two years, Mike is still in touch with the daily happenings at the Brit and hasn't lost touch with his old mates. One of those mates, Steve, owns a box so the three of us wandered up to say hello. A minute later we found ourselves sipping the joyous taste of alcohol for the first time since promotion had been achieved.

It was a bit of a task to get Isabelle into the box (it involved Mike and I hauling her up, one foot each) so when Mum and Dad finally reached us, Mum understandably declined to make her way in! Instead, Isabelle and I wandered into the players bar. Enjoying a beer alongside the boys was quite incredible on such a legendary day. It was a moment I shall cherish for the rest of my life.

So, we had done it! Twenty three years of hurt all over. The season that I can say, "I was there". It truly was magnificent.

It was a moment that will go down as the best in my life.

I will leave local lad Andy Wilkinson to evaluate the season in his own words:

"Promotion, for me, as a home grown player is a dream come true. I was fortunate to have the opportunity to sign for the club I love at 15 years of age. However, I never imagined as I made my way through the academy/youth team, reserves and ultimately into the first team squad that I would be the longest serving player at the club and playing my part in the season where we got promoted to the Premiership.

This means more to me than anyone can appreciate and I owe a lot to the gaffer who believed in me and gave me the chances I needed this season.

I have a great family and friends that support me on and off the pitch which makes it so much more rewarding, so thank you to them!!

The only down side to my season was getting a double hernia after the Newcastle United game which meant me missing out at playing at St. James' Park, but hopefully now there will be more opportunities.

The highlights for me personally to pick a few would be Newcastle United at home where we showed we can more than match it with the Premiership boys and West Brom home and away ('We always beat West Brom!!'). But the ultimate highlight was being in the starting line up in the promotion winning game against Leicester-even though I got injured.

If someone had said to me at the start of the season "you are going to be in the starting line up of the last game of the season but your going to have to go off injured and get stitched up but we are going get promoted"- I would have ripped their hand off!!

It has been a pleasure to play with the lads this season. Our team spirit has been second to none and coupled with the amazing support from our fans there was only one place we were going.

It's a memory that will stay with me forever.

GO ON STOKE!!!"

Wilko sums up everything it means to a Stokie. He takes the spirit of the fans out on to the pitch with him, and promotion clearly meant more to him than anyone.

Andy has come on leaps and bounds since I first saw him ply his trade in the youth sides for the Potters and I am delighted that his hard efforts have culminated in top flight football.

If anybody is looking forward to playing in the biggest stadiums and against the household names in the Premier League, it is this solid defender- well done Mr. Wilkinson, and thank you mate.

"Wilko feeling the burn in pre-season training"

The Aftermath

The day after the night before started off badly. I had the mother of all headaches! The beers from the night before were flashing in my brain and my belly was feeling pretty raw after a Chinese AND a curry. You may as well celebrate in style…

I had to do something Stoke City related. I wandered to the local newsagent to pick up a copy of every national newspaper I could lay my hands on. I was going to get every memento I could from our promotion.

It was then time to call Rob, who explains the events:

"Myself and James ventured down to the Britannia Stadium the day after the day that will forever be remembered as Promotion day. We went into the usually deserted club shop, however on this occasion, we were met by the world's TV and Radio. Stoke City had finally landed as a Premier League team!"

Perfectly put. 'Premier League 08' shirts were on sale, and I ended up queuing for 45 minutes just to get one. It was worth every second. This was history! Beaming smiles were across every single face. Never has such a long queue been so pleasant!

After that we took a stroll right around the ground before heading home ready for tomorrow.

The Tuesday was fantastic. After supping champagne the night before, my head was again rather sore but I didn't care. The sun was out and this was the final chapter in a quite extraordinary season. The victorious players had quite rightly been awarded a Civic Reception and an open top bus tour around the City.

The whole of Stoke-on-Trent and its surrounding suburbs were decked out in red and white. Every car that whizzed past sported a Stoke flag or scarf flying out of the window. Even more incredible was that the handful of people not wearing red and white in fact supported other football clubs. As I saw Chelsea and West Ham shirts I couldn't help but wonder whether our lofty appearance in the league ladder would result in them changing allegiance. What I did know was that this achievement had brought the entire City together.

Dad, Aunty Isabelle, Rob and I took up our position in Bentilee and Snow Hill, Shelton (where Wasim's greasy kebab meat was naturally sampled) to cheer the boys before travelling to the main event at the Britannia Stadium.

A quite incredible season had ended in the sweetest possible way. As the boys were paraded around the pitch, receiving the adulation of about 14,000 Stokies, I afforded myself a smile.

Tony Pulis had shut up all his critics and the unfashionable Stoke City will next season be lining up against The Champions of Europe in a League fixture.

My arm was taking a battering as I kept pinching myself. It was all true.

The perfect ending to a perfect season.

Thank you Stoke.

"Ecstasy!"

"Aunty Isabelle, Mike and the author on the pitch"

"The pitch is well and truly invaded!"

"Me and Mike in the box!"

"Dad, me and Mike on a historic day"

"We are Premier League!"

"The triumphant bus tour"

"Bentilee goes crazy!"